The *Vivendier*

Frontispiece: the Kassel manuscript, part of f° 163v.
(The image has been scanned and imperfections removed.)

THE
VIVENDIER

*"Chy commenche un vivendier et ordonnance
pour appariller pluiseurs manierez de viandes"*

A CRITICAL EDITION
WITH ENGLISH TRANSLATION

by
Terence Scully

PROSPECT BOOKS
1997

Published in Great Britain by Prospect Books in 1997,
at Allaleigh House, Blackawton, Totnes, Devon TQ9 7DL, England.

©1997, Terence Scully.
The translator and editor, Terence Scully, asserts his right to be identified as translator and editor of this work in accordance with the Copyright, Designs & Patents Act 1988.

No part of this publication may be reproduced, stored in a retrieval system, or transmitted in any form or by any means, electronic, mechanical, photo-copying, recording or otherwise, without the prior permission of the copyright holder.

British Library Cataloguing in Publication Data:
A catalogue entry of this book is available from the British Library.

Typeset by Terence Scully.

Cataloguing-in-publication data
Scully, Terence
The Vivendier
ISBN 0907325815
1. Cookery, French—Early works to 1800. I. Scully, Terence, 1935– .
II. Title. III. The Vivendier.

ISBN 0 907325 815

Printed by Antony Rowe Ltd, Bumper's Farm, Chippenham, Wiltshire.

Table of Contents

I. Introduction 1

  A. The Manuscript 1

    (i) Physical description and date of the manuscript 1
    (ii) Contents of the manuscript 2
    (iii) The *Vivendier* 5
      (a) Dialect 5
        1. Phonology 6
        2. Vocabulary 9
        3. Grammar 10
      (b) Date and place of origin of the *Vivendier* 11

  B. The Recipes in the *Vivendier* 13

    (i) Composition of this collection 13
    (ii) Other French recipe collections 14
    (iii) Sources used for the *Vivendier* 16

  C. The Cookery of the *Vivendier* 23

    (i) The kitchen and its utensils 23
    (ii) Ingredients 24
    (iii) Other observations 27

  D. Editorial Principles 28

**II. The *Vivendier*. Original Text with Translation
     and Commentary on the Recipes and Cookery** . 31

III. Ingredients and Glossary 95

  A. Ingredients in the Recipes 95

  B. Glossary of the Recipes 97

❖ v ❖

IV. Appendices **107**

   A. Table of the Recipes in the *Vivendier*
           and Concordances in the *Enseignements* and *Viandier*   107

   B. Juxtaposition of the *Vivendier*, the *Viandier* and the *Enseignements*   109

   C. *Contre pestilence*   120

   D. Summary Bibliography   128

❖

I. Introduction

A. The Manuscript

(i) Physical description and date of the manuscript

A detailed description of the manuscript of the Gesamthochschul-Bibliothek Kassel, 4° Ms. med. 1, can be read in the Library's catalogue: *Die Handscriften der murhardschen Bibliothek der Stadt Kassel und Landesbibliothek.* Band 3, 1: *Manuscripta medica. Herausgegeben von Dieter Hennig*, Wiesbaden (Otto Harrassowitz), 1976, pp. 19–23.

> Französische Sammelhandschrift: Aldobrandino de Sienne · Taillevent · Jacques Despars · Jean Pitard · Medizinische, alchemistische und astrologische Texte. Papier · 396 Bl. · 21x14 · Nordfrankreich · um 1430–1475.

The cataloguer, Hartmut Broszinski, identifies three distinct "volumes" that have been bound together in this codex.[1] He has recorded a variety of watermarks in the manuscript's paper: an anchor (attested in Picardy, 1426–31); a coat-of-arms (*c.* 1470); a unicorn (1440–44); a sprite (1421–44); a letter "Y" (*c.* 1472). All of these are in the first part of the manuscript, the part that contains the *Vivendier* although, perhaps significantly, none can be seen specifically in the gathering occupied by the *Vivendier*.

There are no horizontal guidelines drawn on the pages to help the scribe. Likewise there are no lines, vertical or horizontal, drawn to indicate the limits of the script on a page and so to define the margins.

The manuscript contains no illuminations. In the gathering that is devoted primarily to the *Vivendier*, however, a rubricator at some time used a very moderate amount of red ink to enhance capitals, and to insert punctuation slashes and the dots that distinguish roman numerals.

The folios throughout the manuscript are numbered in two of three series. The first gathering, ff° 1–15v, shows roughly formed roman numerals to the right of centre at the top of each recto. This gathering contains the table of contents for the

---

[1] "Die Hs. (Ergänzungsschrift) ist zusammengesetzt aus 3 Teilen: Bl. 1–250 u. 383–396; 251–296; 297–382." Bruno Laurioux has also compiled a description of the Kassel manuscript in his *Le règne de Taillevent. Livres et pratiques culinaires à la fin du Moyen Âge*, Paris (Publications de la Sorbonne), 1997, pp. 361–2.

whole volume,[2] and an apparently incidental filler on the *Proprietees du poullieul* drawn from the *Macer floribus*; it ends with a blank page, Then, beginning with a large, bold .i. on f° 16r, the main series of roman numerals identifies each of the remaining folios in the manuscript; they are placed in the centre top of the recto pages, but wherever a rubric appears centred in this area, the numeral is displaced to the left. There seem to be at least two errors in that enumeration[3]; they are the numbers referred to in the table of contents. A third, apparently accurate numbering, in a modern hand in arabic numerals, was placed in the top right corner of the recto pages. It is of this last numbering that we and the library catalogue make use.

On f° 1r of the manuscript, someone, presumably an owner, has inscribed several words which include a name: *Exitus acta probat / Jo de herzelles aliarn / seding Cappellany*.[4] The catalogue identifies the patronymic as relating to Herzele in East Flanders.

(ii) Contents of the manuscript

The Kassel manuscript contains a miscellany of medical and botanical information, and household and personal advice. Some forty discrete sections follow one another here. The most important of these, in terms of the number of folios they occupy, are 31 folios containing some 100 recipes for distilled waters ... *qui li anchyen filosofe firent*; 75 folios of Aldobrandino's *Regime du corps*; 31 folios of medical recipes; 27 folios excepted from the *Circa instans*, in French; 21 folios on the four Complections; 31 folios of alchemical recipes, including distillations. Also inserted, here and there among these more substantial pieces are several further, briefer series of medical recipes; four folios of a *Secreta mulierum*, in French; four folios on phlebotomy; twelve folios excerpted from the *Livre du tresor*; six folios of surgical recipes; six folios on urinalysis; seven folios of descriptions of the

---

[2] The recipe collection which begins on f° 140 (original foliation) is not identified with any particular name in the table of contents. For that folio the scribe has written merely *Pour savoir apareillier plusieurz manieres de viandes et premiez Pour une barbe Robert*.

[3] The folio numbers jump from *lx* to *lxii*; two consecutive folios are numbered *cxci*, although later correctly labelled *205* and *206*.

[4] The first phrase is proverbial and found first in Ovid's *Heroides*, 2, 85: "The event justifies the deed." DuCange (2, 122a) glosses the word *capellani* as "*denique sequioribus sæculis vocati, qui capellis, sacellis, seu ædiculis sacris, præfacti sunt*" — that is, chaplains. At the same place is an entry for the phrase *capellanus altaris*. In the inscribed text the second letter of *aliar*... has the length of an *l* but also has a high crossbar of a *t*. The final "letter" may be a rough abbreviation for *us* or *cum* and is capped with a superscript slur. The word which appears as *seding* (of which the *g* is quite neat) is likely *sedinus*; this spelling may perhaps represent a version of *sedilium* or *sedilis*, "throne, episcopal see" (Niermeyer, 954a). See DuCange, 7, 397b: *sedinus*.

❖ I. Introduction ❖

planets; and, remarkably, recurrent instances of plague *regimine*, in various styles and of various lengths. In one case the compiler duplicates a plague text that has already been copied. With very few exceptions, all of this material is in French. In this regard it is noteworthy that relatively learned, scientific material, traditionally preserved and transmitted in Latin, has been copied here uniformly in vernacular translations.

The series of culinary recipes which are of present interest is located between folios 154r and 164v (inclusive). Apart from f° 153 (recto and verso), which precedes it, the *Vivendier* occupies the whole of a gathering. Beginning at two-thirds of the way down f° 162v, a new hand has squeezed additional recipes into what remained of blank pages in the gathering.

Although the modern catalogue of the manuscript identifies this series of recipes as "*Guillaume Tirel dit Taillevent: le Viandier*," the collection of 66 recipes is only partially and indirectly related to *le Viandier*. The *incipit* that is copied immediately ahead of the recipes reads, *Chy commenche un vivendier et ordonnance pour apparillier pluiseurs manierez de viandes.* However, the term *vivendier* may be misleading for the modern reader who knows of the work connected with Taillevent's name. It is important to realize that the indefinite article, *un*, which precedes the term in our manuscript indicates that the author felt his compilation to be generic rather than a copy or adaptation of the famous *le Viandier*.[5] The pages of culinary recipes take their place alongside other pages of other practical and "scientific" information gleaned by the manuscript's compiler from a wide variety of sources. The preceding folios contain Aldobrandino de Siena's *Regime du corps*, whose last paragraphs are given over, significantly, to an extensive exposition of food properties: *Pour savoir la nature dez chars que on use et desquelles on doit user*; *Pour savoir la nature de le char de porc, ... de buef, ... de breby, ... de mouton, ... dez oysiaulx, ... de gelines, ... de cock.*

Immediately preceding and following the series of culinary recipes are two works attributed to a single author, a certain physician by the name of Jacques Despars. Although the manuscript offers no information on this person, a good deal is in fact known about him.[6] He appears to have been very highly respected in both

---

[5] The copies of this latter work that are now in the Paris Bibliothèque Nationale and the Biblioteca Vaticana bear a definite article in their *incipit*: *Cy comence le Viandier Taillevent* .... Even without explicitly attaching Taillevent's name to it, we now automatically privilege his version of the collection by calling it *le Viandier*.

[6] For a brief biographical sketch of Jacques Despars see Earnest Wickersheimer, *Dictionnaire biographique des médecins en France au moyen âge*, 2 vols., repr. of the 1936 edn., Geneva (Droz), 1979; I, pp. 326–7. For a more thorough study see Danielle Jacquart, "Le regard d'un médecin sur son temps: Jacques Despars (1380?–1458),"

medical and academic circles in his day. The first piece credited to Dr. Despars and copied into this manuscript is brief. It is advice on relieving an overful stomach — curiously, perhaps facetiously, appropriate advice, given the nature of the material that will be copied on the subsequent folios. The text seems to serve as a filler for the bottom third of f° 153v after the conclusion of Aldobrandino's long treatise. It is not mentioned in the table of contents, having apparently been added after the table was compiled.

> Pour conforter l'estommacque quant on est trop renpli, et que on a trop court alaine — et ce du conseille maistre Jaque Despars, docteur en medechine.[7]
>
> Prenés ung petit de alewe, une louchié de feneule et une louchié de coreiande preparee, et mettre en .i. pot et le boulir avecque .i. lot d'eauwe tant que il reviegne a demilot; et en boire du matin en jun chacun jour .i. voire et le continuer pour .v. ou .vi. jours.
>
> To comfort the stomach when it is too full, and one is too short of breath — on the advice of Master Jacques Despars, Medical Doctor.
>
> Take a little aloes, a spoonful of fennel and a spoonful of prepared coriander, put them into a pot with a measure of water to boil until half has boiled away; drink a glassful of this on an empty stomach every morning over five or six days.

Following the folios devoted to the food recipes, on ff° 165r–166v at the opening of the next gathering, is a second work attributed to Doctor Jacques Despars. This is a longer and more serious disquisition, one belonging to a well recognized fourteenth- and fifteenth-century genre having to do with ways to avoid an infection of the plague or to check its effects.

> Contre pestilence du conseil maistre Jaque des pars[8]
>
> Pour se preserver de pestilence on se doit garder de toutes choses qui eschaufent le sanc, comme font sel, salures fortes, espices, fortes saulses, aux, ognons, poriaus, moustarde, fors vins, claré, ypocras, ...

Bibliothèque de l'Ecole des Chartes, 138 (1980), pp. 35–86. A native of Tournai, he taught in the medical faculty at the University of Paris from 1411 to 1419, then practised and wrote in Tournai or Cambrai until 1450. He served the Duke of Burgundy in both the capacities of physician and counsellor. His major work, a commentary on the *Liber canonis* of Avicenna, was widely copied by medical students at Paris and by colleagues, particularly in the north of France and in the Lowlands.

[7] ms.: *medech.*, with a superscript slur over the second syllable. This sentence is indented, and is intended as a rubric for the following paragraph.

[8] The beginning of this rubric is indented, as if to centre it on the page. Before these first words, in a different hand, has been inserted the phrase, *Pour se garder*. Because much of the advice contained in these paragraphs deals with culinary or alimentary matters, the entire piece is reproduced in Appendix C, below.

❖ I. Introduction ❖ 5

The contents of the manuscript appear to have been selected because they offer both authoritative and practical counsel on living well and safely. On the whole, the codex would seem to be of most immediate usefulness to a medical practitioner. It is most likely to have been compiled at the instigation of a physician, and probably for his personal ownership and consultation. He would thus have ensured himself of ready access to reference material in his professional practice. The compiler must have felt that the series of food recipes that he selected and bound among all these scientific (and pseudo-scientific) resources belonged there and enriched his collection. In fact, the association between culinary and medical information was firmly established in late-medieval thinking.[9]

(iii) The *Vivendier*

(a) Dialect

A linguistic study of the text of the *Vivendier* as this is written in the Kassel manuscript can be organized along three lines: phonological, lexical and grammatical. In each case what is particularly useful to observe are those features that constitute exceptions to the normal state of "French" in the late Middle Ages.[10] A reference to a linguistic authority is made wherever that authority relates a peculiarity to the dialect(s) of north-eastern France.

The authorities cited here are the following:

Mildred K. Pope, *From Latin to Modern French with Especial Consideration of Anglo-Norman. Phonology and Morphology*, Manchester (Manchester University Press), 1934.

Walther von Wartburg, *Evolution et structure de la langue française*, 5th edn., Bern (A. Francke), 1958; "La Picardie," pp. 86–88.

---

[9] It is not unusual to find recipes and recipe collections copied along with medical material. The original French text of the *Enseignements*, for instance, appears in a collection of medical-surgical works (today in the Bibliothèque National of Paris, latin 7131) which dates from the beginning of the fourteenth century; a Latin translation of this same assortment of recipes, titled *Doctrine preparationis ciborum*, is found also in the same sort of volume of medical miscellanea, but one which was likely compiled around 1370 (Biblioteca Apostolica Vaticana, Palatino latino 1179). See Carole Lambert, *Trois réceptaires culinaires médiévaux: les Enseingnemenz, les Doctrine et le Modus. Edition critique et glossaire détaillé*, unpublished Ph.D. Thesis, Université de Montréal, 1989, 27–9 and 33–4; and Melitta Weiss-Amer, "The Role of Medieval Physicians in the Diffusion of Culinary Recipes and Cooking Practices," *Du manuscrit à la table*, ed. Carole Lambert, Montréal (Presses de l'Université de Montréal), 1992, 69–80.

[10] Where the location in our text of the following words and phrases is not indicated, by means of the recipe numbers in which they occur, they may be found by referring to the Glossary (below), or may be understood to occur relatively frequently in the text.

❖ The *Vivendier* ❖

Edouard Bourciez, *Eléments de linguistique romane*, 4th edn., Paris (Klincksieck), 1956.

Pierre Fouché, *Phonétique historique du français*, 3 vols., Paris (Klincksieck), 1961.

Christiane Marchello-Nizia, *Histoire de la langue française aux XIVe et XVe siècles*, Paris (Bordas), 1979.

Gunnar Tilander, *Glanures lexicographiques*, Lund, London, Oxford, Paris, Leipzig (Gleerup, Milford, Oxford University, Droz, Harrassowitz), 1932.

Furthermore, the *Anglo-Norman Dictionary*, ed. Louise W. Stone, William Rothwell and T. B. W. Reid, London (Modern Humanities Research Association), 1977–92, casts light on several exceptional forms, as does the *Dictionnaire de l'ancienne langue française* of Frédéric Godefroy.

1. Phonology

The most obvious phonetic particularities of the *Vivendier*'s text are found in areas of the gutturals, the palatals and certain vowel sounds. Other traits, which we shall list below, may also have some significance and help place the text geographically.

i) The guttural sounds, *k* and *g*, show some resistance to being affected by the middle vowel *a* (Wartburg, §§1 and 2): *cappon, roques* (for *roches*), *becquet, muscades, broque* (rather than *broche, brochet*), *lesques* (for Francian *leches*) 61, *blanque* (feminine) 61, 65, *gaune* 61, and *caut* (for *chaut*) 65.

ii) The language of the text shows a relatively strong tendency to retain a palatal before a front vowel. While in most cases in Francian a consonant would have passed to a more dental sibilant, our text shows a sound further back on the palate (Wartburg, §3; Bourciez, §269, a; Fouché, p. 923): *chy commenche* in the *incipit* of the work, *tronchons* (for *tronçons*, from **truncionem*), *pieches, despechier* and *despeschier* (for *pieces* and *despec(i)er*), *dreschier* (< *directiare*), *forche* 66. A gutteral is likewise palatalized: *chucquere, fresce* fem. 17. In the last syllable of *esgoutier* 29 (a form of the verb which appears to be unattested in any dictionary), the dental seems to be palatalized before a front vowel. The form *arge* (a third-person singular subjunctive of *ardre*: *ardeat*) similarly represents a palatalization of a dental (voiced), the equivalent of the Francian *arse*; Froissart uses this same form *arge*.[11]

---

[11] August Scheler, ed., *Œuvres de Froissart*, 3 vols., Brussels (Devaux), 1870–72; Vol. 3, p. 314.

❖ I. Introduction ❖   7

The presence of a palatal tends in turn to close a vowel (Pope, §1320, xviii and §1322, ii): *gitter* (for *jeter*) 63, *apparilliez* (for *appareillez*) 33, *hechiet* (for *haché*) 62. A yod is maintained following a palatal consonant (Bourciez, §264, a): the last two examples, *apparilliez, hechiet*, as well as *despechier, dreschier, mengier, refroidier, saignier, sechier* and *trenchier*. As a result of the same influence, even a back vowel such as *o* is occasionally closed by a palatal: *bruyerés* (for *broyerés*) 61, and *buillon* (for *bouillon*) 62.

In a final position, a sibilant or a palatalized guttural, which may be a velar fricative, does not fall but is represented by means of the spelling *ch* (Bourciez, §290): *luchs, coulich, tierch* 15 (the form *tiers* is also written), and *douch* (as in *sain douch*) 66.

The palatal semi-vowel is sensed to be a semi-consonant, as the spelling of the word *vergus* shows it consistently up to Recipe 57, although the forms *verius, vertius* and *vierius* replace that spelling from Recipe 61 onwards.

iii) Among the liquids and sibilants, the replacement of a pre-consonantal *s* by *r* is a Picard tendency (Pope, §378, i): the form *harlé* occurs in seven instances (in place of *haslé*). The sound *r* is substituted for *l*: *garentine* (for *galentine*), *connir* for *conil* (neither form with *r* is attested in any Old French dictionary, although the *Anglo-Norman Dictionary* shows the *conier*).

Of the sibilants, *s* tends likewise to be persistent before a consonant even though it is at the end of a syllable within a word (Pope, §1321, xiii): *esbrocher, escaille, eschauder, eslire, estamine, estamper, estoupes, estremper, esve* and *esventrer*. Similarly, the *s* persists in a palatal group: *fresce, dreschier* and *despeschier*.

Under the influence of *l*, a final *s* is voiced (Pope, §378, commenting on Anglo-Norman orthography): *fillez* 51.

Under the pen of the *Vivendier*'s scribe, the letter *l* shows with remarkable consistency what may be either an incomplete vocalization before a consonant or merely an orthographic habit[12]: *aultre, chault, fault, hault* 59, *eulx* (modern *œufs*), *moyelx, moyeulx, mieulx, morceaulx, oysiaulz, pouldre, pourldre, poreaulx, saulse, saulsices, peult* 65, *voelt* 25, 31, 61, 66, *veolt* 61, *veulx, veult, vouldrez*. In either case the practice is likely not dialectal. Concerning the forms *soultil* 23 and *dessoulz* 58, however, Godefroy presents several illustrations (respectively 7, 564a and b; and 7, 548b for the verb *soulzester*) which relate them to north-eastern regions.

---

[12] See Charles Beaulieux, *Histoire de l'orthographie française*, 2 vols., Paris (Champion), 1927; Vol. 1, p. 181.

iv) Miscellaneous consonants:

A final *t* is retained in northern and north-eastern dialects (Pope 1320, xv and §1322, vi; Bourciez, §275, c): *quantitet* 61, *moitiet* 62, *crut* 62, and the past participles in *ara estet, aroset, boulit* 66.

A glide consonant is not generated where Francian would do so (Pope, §1320, xiii; Wartburg, §4): *poure* (for *poudre* and *pouldre*) 48, 61 (four times), 65, *vaura* 58.

Intervocalic *w* is persistent (Pope, §1321 (xi)): *keuwe* 15; and a *w* is generated from the intervocalic group *qu* (Pope, §1321, xii): *yauwe, yawe, auwe* variously in 61-66.

In northern dialects, [*o*] (from *en le*) was raised to [*u*] (Pope, §843): *ou* (a digraph) as in *ou plus gras* 27, *ou moillon* 30, *ou temps d'esté* 51, *ou lieu de* 66, *mettre ou pasté* 66; and in the prepositional phrase *ens ou*[13]: *ens ou plat, ens ou pasté, en ou four* 53, 59, 62, 65, 66.

v) Among the vowel sounds, the unstressed feminine definite article *la* tends to reduce to a *le* (Pope, §1320, xii): *le viande, le louche, le poudre, le sause, de le moustarde, le blanque,* 65.

vi) Where diphthongs and triphthongs involve a strongly accented element, they tend to simplify, a feature of northern and north-eastern dialects. Our text consistently has *ly* for *lui* (Pope, §1250, ii) as the third person dative pronoun.

The diphthong *ai* is reduced to *a* (Bourciez, §264, b): *char* (there are thirteen instances of this; the Francian form *chair* is not written in the text).

In particular the feminine *e* following a yod and a stressed *e* is dropped (that is, *ié+e > ié*) (Pope, §1320, v and §1322, iii): *char hachié, char cuitte et mengié, char despechié, une broche delié, petittes louchiés* 66, and *grosse dragié* 16.

Similarly (cf. Pope, §1250, i) the triphthong *uié* has a form without the medial element: *essuer* 50, 51, 57. The diphthong [*u+e*] becomes [*o+e*]: *roelles* 21, *noef* 30, 46, *voelt* 25, 3, 61, 66.[14] The forms *bure* or *burre* (written thus on 13 occasions in our text, for *beure* or *beurre* which do not occur) is attested in the *Anglo-Norman Dictionary* alone.

---

[13] In the *Cantilène de sainte Eulalie* (tenth century) the earliest form of this phrase exists already: *enz enl fou*.

[14] The study by Gilles Roques — "La conjugaison du verbe *vouloir* en ancien français," in Anthonij Dees, ed., *Actes du IVe Colloque international sur le moyen français*, Amsterdam (Rodolpi), 1985, pp. 227-265 — relates the form *voelt* (a case of a "diphthong without vocalization" according to the author) to the fifteenth century and to the Picard dialect: the author's illustrations are drawn from the *Passion de Mons* (in Hainaut) and Jean Froissart (b. Valenciennes).

In our text the first element of the thriphthong *eau* tends to close: *iau* (Pope, §1320, viii; Wartburg, §6): *nouviaux, poriaus, yauwe* (as well as *yawe, yauw*). Similarly the first element of the complex compound of *moyeulx* (yolks) tightens into *mieulx* 62.

The diphthong *ou* occurs as *au* (Bourciez, §265): *claux (de ginofle)* 66.

vii) Spellings and orthographic preferences:

The enclitic form *as* 66 (for *aux*), common in early Old French was retained late in Anglo-Norman (Pope, §1252, ii).

The spelling *gh* is used to represent a [g] before a front vowel (Pope, §701): *langhe, mughettes, hongherie*.

The use of the letter *k*, while *lettre morte* in standard French, is relatively common in Froissart. The *Vivendier*'s word *keuwe* 15 (for *queue*) appears almost identically as *keuve* in Froissart.[15] The citations of this form of the word in Tobler-Lommatsch (2, col. 518–21) tend to be northern.

viii) Verb forms:

The verb *fraier* remains *froyé* 5 (< *fricare*), a form that appears in the *Anglo-Norman Dictionary*. The form *loie* 59 (the French infinitive *lier*) also appears; Froissart uses the form *loier* rather than the Francian *lier*.[16]

The form *poés* 66 for the second person plural of *pooir* is found identically in Froissart.[17]

The imperfect subjunctive of *estre* has the north-eastern form *fuist* for the third person singular in Recipe 62 (see Bourciez, §295, b; the form is attested also in Anglo-Norman: Pope, §§1160, 1238).

The imperative of *prendre* remains *prendés* (61, 62, 63, 65, 66) in northern regions (Pope, §937).

2. Vocabulary:

A word in the *Vivendier* for a variety of cooking pan, *telle* 27, 44, is recognized by Godefroy (7, 662c); his illustrations are drawn solely from the towns of Douai (near Valenciennes, in Hainaut) and Tournai (near Lille), and from the *Menagier de Paris* (ed. Pichon, Vol. 2, p. 276) where the word appears among the supplementary

---

[15] Ed. Scheler, Vol. 3, p. 366.

[16] Rob Roy McGregor, ed., *The Lyric Poems of Jehan Froissart: a Critical Edition*, Chapel Hill (Department of Romance Languages, University of North Carolina), 1975; p. 344.

[17] Auguste Longnon, ed., *Méliador par Jean Froissart*, 3 vols., Paris (Firman Didot), 1895–99; Vol. 3, p. 313.

material provided by *Hotin le quisenier qui fu a Monseigneur de Roubais*; Roubais is a town near Lille.

mughettez, muscades The scribe writes *pau* and *pauch* 59, 64 (in standard French *peu*): the *FEW* (8, 51a) relates the form *pau* to *alütt* - i.e. Old *Liégeois*.

Tobler-Lommatsch (9, col. 62) has two examples of the word *saille* 9, 10, both of which are of northern French origin. In his article *saille (nostree)*, 'la sauge', Tilander (pp. 233–34) refers to Hécart, *Dictionnaire rouchi* (that is, of the Hainaut region) and to L. Vermesse, *Vocabulaire du patois lillois* showing north-eastern use of the term *saille*.

The preposition *ens*, which is cited by Marchello-Nizia[18] as having virtually disappeared in standard Middle French, is used five times among the last recipes of the *Vivendier* (59, 62, 65 and 66); in only one earlier instance it is an adverb: *Quant tout est ens . . .* 30.

Godefroy (*s.v. roche*) offers one example of the form *rocques* for the fish roach; it is from Tournai in 1464.

Godefroy's two examples (4, 114a) of the verb *fourbouillir* 64, 66, are from Flanders and from Lille (in 1480). Godefroy also notes that the term *fourbouillir* continues to live in modern Rouchi — that is, in the dialect spoken around Valenciennes. It has the same medieval sense of "to parboil", although with a rather limited application: "blanchir des légumes, des herbages."

A hesitation is curious in the form of *œuf* which is spelled with an *f* or an *l*: *oef, oeufs, oels, oeus, oex*; and, likewise, the "mid-egg" or yolk: *moioeufs, mioefz, moefz, moyelx, moyeulx, moyeux*. It is not clear whether the forms with *l* are dialectal or merely, in the orthographic domain, represent a false etymological restoration of that letter because of the palatal vowel that could be thought to derive distantly from a vocalization.

The word *esve*, from the Latin *aqua*, is by far the preferred form for our author or scribe, who writes it a remarkable 26 times. This form seems to be unattested in any Old French dictionary. In our text its use is limited to the first part of the collection, though, up to Recipe 52; from Recipe 58 onwards that form is replaced by variations of the standard French *eaue*.

3. Grammar

Adverbial -*s* is rare by the fifteenth century. Although the adverb *premiers* 1, "at first, firstly," is an exceptional survivor from Old French, Godefroy's citations of the

---

[18] At p. 271, the author identifies this word *ens* as an adverb in Old French, and states that it "est fort rarement utilisé comme préposition en moyen français, et presque toujours au sens temporel." All six occurrences of the word in our text are, however, spacial rather than temporal.

word (6, 281b and c) tend to be from northern sources. Our text has a form *premiés* 63, as well. Froissart makes use of *premiers* to the exclusion of *premierement*.[19] The adverb *meismes* 42 (*si qu'il se puist escumer de lui meismes*) also appears.

The singular *vo* is used (rather than *vostre* (Wartburg, §11; Bourciez, §306, c): *vo goust* 1, *vo lievre* 64 (twice), 66, *vo potage* 64.

(b) Date and place of origin of the *Vivendier*

According to the language of the various texts in this recipe collection, we should locate this copy in the north, and most likely in the north-east, of France. Whether the precise origin of the copy was Artois (the region around Arras, nowdays the *département* of the Pas de Calais) or Picardy (whose capital was Amiens), or Hainaut (around Valenciennes, with its *rouchi* dialect), the dialect that flavours the copy seems most to possess those linguistic features recognized as being peculiar to that general locality of the north east. This dialect shows only one or two obvious signs of exclusively Walloon characteristics (that is, of the Liège area). Only incidentally do its linguistic features reflect what is typical of Norman or Anglo-Norman usage.

The juxtaposition with the *Vivendier* of two pieces by a single highly respected physician, whose home was in the Cambrai-Tournai area, suggests that the manuscript's compiler was not only a fellow physician but a compatriot of Doctor Jacques Despars. Furthermore, as was mentioned earlier, someone, presumably an early owner of the manuscript, has put his name on the initial folio. It has been suggested that this Jo de Herzelles is related to the town of Herzele in East Flanders.

When we come later to examine the nature of the foodstuffs that enter into these recipes, we shall observe that there is a preference for dairy products and for sea-fish. There is no fresh grape juice (must) in the recipes, although some use is made of wine and much use of vinegar.[20] There is no use of large game animals, but only of rabbit and hare. These ingredients point to the home of this compilation of recipes being in the north and perhaps north-east of France, in flat grain-growing or dairy lands, without extensive wildlands and within easy transportation distance of

---

[19] Ed. Scheler.

[20] At the time of the *Vivendier*, this wine may well have been from a local source: in his commentary on Avicenna's *Canon*, Jacques Despars notes the planting of grape vines in Brabant and especially around Amiens and Cambrai (see Jacquart, "Le regard d'un médecin," p. 48). Vinegar was, of course, easier than wine or verjuice to keep on hand over a relatively long period of time without it deteriorating. The name of the substance is usually written in our text as two words, *vin aigre* or *vin esgre*, as if the writer were particularly conscious of the origin of the product.

sea.[21] By the middle of the fifteenth century the northern domains of Charles the Bold of Burgundy included Hainaut, Flanders, Artois and Picardy. The household in which our compilation was assembled may have been sensitive to the influence of the glorious Burgundian court.[22]

The presence immediately before and immediately after our group of recipes of texts attributed to Dr. Jacques Despars helps to suggest a date and locale for the copy of the recipes. (See Note 6, above.) The first of the doctor's texts (*Pour conforter l'estommacque* ...) was copied on the *verso* of the first folio of the gathering that contains the *Vivendier* (at f° 153v), so that we must think that the beginning of the series of recipes was probably copied at about the same time. Master Jacques Despars is not unknown in history. He was, in fact, an individual of some repute, enjoying an appointment as chief physician to King Charles VII of France (r. 1422–61). He was born in Tournai in about 1380, was educated in arts and medicine at Paris, and in 1406 was elected Rector of the University of Paris. In 1427 and at other times he served professionally in the House of Burgundy, and toward the end of his life was named to prebends from churches in Cambrai, Cuvillers (near Cambrai), Tournai and Cysoing (near Tournai). He died in 1458. He was very much a celebrity of that region.

The date of this copy of the *Vivendier* would appear to be close to that of the manuscript compilation itself, that is to say very roughly the middle of the fifteenth century.

❖

---

[21] A maximum distance for the transportation of fresh sea-fish at this time was roughly 150 kilometers.

[22] The *Mémoires d'Olivier de la Marche, maître d'hôtel et capitaine des gardes de Charles le Téméraire* (ed. Henri Beaune and J. D'Arbaumont, 4 vols., Paris: Renouard, 1883–88) mention a number of banquets arranged by both the Duke and various of his noble vassals in the northern lands: Lille, 1443 (*joustes et grans festiemens*: Vol. II, p. 56); Lille, 1450 (*joustes et tournoiemens*: II, 211); Mons in Hainaut, May 1451 (the celebrated *Feste de la Toison d'Or*: II, 204ff. and 368ff.); Lille, January–February 1453 (where the Duke and Duchess *faisoient banquets, joustes, tournois et festiemens grans et pompeulx*: II, 333); Cambray, March 1454 (the *Feste de la Licorne* ... *ou il y eut tournois et joustes, et grans entremetz*); Lille, November 1464 (III, 4); and so forth.

B. The Recipes of the *Vivendier*

(i) Composition of this collection

The *Vivendier* contains 66 recipes. This count is of the paragraphs which are regularly set off from one recipe to the next by means of a narrow blank space, and by the scribe's use of a larger initial capital to mark the beginning of a recipe. The first words of a recipe, furthermore, often employ a formula that embodies the name of the dish — for example, *Pour faire brouet de vergus* .... However, the reader may make subdivisions within a recipe, perceiving two or more discrete recipes following a single "title". In a few cases, for instance, where the writer offers variations to modify the colour or flavour of a dish, or substitutes one major ingredient for another, we might have considered that the passage in question constitutes a new and distinct recipe. Such does not seem to have been the writer's intention, though.

The recipes selected for this compilation are an assortment that represents a variety of genres. The arrangement of the recipes is not clearly deliberate. Their sequence occasionally groups several dishes of the same type, but in only two places do rubrics actually identify a "chapter" of dishes that reasonably belong together. Otherwise, the placement of the recipes in the order that they follow in this collection might, *prima facie*, be thought to be random.[23]

The *Vivendier* begins with a sauce (Recipe 1) followed by dishes for eel, poached eggs and venison (2–4); then there is a so-called *pasté*, which is not a pie, another sauce, a rich, sweet custard and devilled eggs (5–8); a grouping of three recipes for meats follows (9–11), and then another of three pastry dishes (12–14); the next two recipes (15–16), although different — one is a tour-de-force for cooking a single fish in three different ways, and the other is a sweet dish of sops — seem to be diversionary preparations[24]; the following grouping of three recipes (17–19) may be intended to afford resort when a sickdish is needed; a relatively long section is composed of a series of six *brouets* (20–25); the five recipes that come afterwards (26–30) may be associated because they are for lean dishes, but generically each is quite different from the others. The first rubric, *Chapittre de poissons*, introduces five recipes for fish. The second rubric, *Chapittre de saulces*, introduces six sauces, neatly arranged — again in groups of three — in two series of "unboiled" (*i.e.* cold:

---

[23] For a table of the contents of the *Vivendier* by recipe name and position, see Appendix A, below.

[24] Such impressive and amusing "incidentals" are properly called *entremets* in early French cuisine.

36–38) and boiled (39–41) sauces. Then the scribe has copied recipes for crayfish and lamprey (42–44), for mutton, peas and beans (45–47), and for sops for Lent made again of peas (48). There follow a pseudo-rice dish, an actual rice dish and one for vermicelli (49–51); six pottages (with, and for use on, a variety of foodstuffs: 52–56; the last, remarkably, involves snails) conclude the first of the two distinct sections in the compilation.

The book's second section is evidently composed of material appended after the first copyist had finished his work, leaving several blank pages in the gathering. It begins with three recipes (58–60) that could quite clearly have been headed *entremets*; the third one has barely more than the title, and there breaks off, unfinished: most likely the scribe-compiler realized that the book already contained directions for preparing this *entremets* at Recipe 15; besides, he had arrived at the foot of a page, f° 163r. The concluding six recipes (61–66) are a miscellany in themselves: a sauce, with variations; a liver sauce for capon; an onion sauce for cooked eggs; hare stew; chick pies; and, finally, a *reprise*, with variations and amplifications, of the hare stew just written out.

This compilation of recipes is clearly a unicum, assembled, over time, from a variety of sources. Its owner(s)/compiler(s) has (have) appended material as the occasion arose, without being overly concerned about the order of the contents or any uniformity of prose style.

(ii) Other French recipe collections

French recipe collections in the vernacular date from a period around 1300. The earliest two of these "books" are the *Enseignements* and the first known copy of the work that will become known as the *Viandier*.[25] The *Enseignements* is extant in only one copy, although it is echoed in the Latin translation, *Doctrine preparationis ciborum*, mentioned above; it presents an assortment of some 53 recipes for large cuts of meat, prepared dishes and fish. The Valais recipe collection, a double-sided manuscript roll, marks a great step forward over the other book, containing as it does some 169 recipes which are organized more carefully and presented in a somewhat more professional style.

Thereafter, further subsequent versions of the Valais collection become known as the *Viandier*. These versions, three in number now although others are known to have existed but been lost or destroyed, subsist from the fourteenth and fifteen centuries. As well, the *Menagier de Paris*, written in the 1390s and extant today in

---

[25] For information on modern editions of the works mentioned here, see the Bibliography in Appendix D, below. For an exhaustive study of the various manuscripts containing these works, see Bruno Laurioux, *Le Règne de Taillevent* mentioned in Note 1, above.

❖ I. Introduction ❖ 15

several copies, contains a long section of food recipes that is itself to a significant degree derived from the *Viandier*.

Written in a Latin that embodies numerous lapses into a Provençal dialect, the modest, late-fourteenth-century *Modus viaticorum preparandorum et salsarum* combines standard "French" dishes with others whose origin seems rather to be Catalan.[26]

In 1420 Chiquart wrote his *Du fait de cuisine* which affords the best and most detailed presentation of the professional activities of a late-medieval cook in a noble household. After 1466 an anonymous compiler assembled his own recipe assortment that became known, after the sole manuscript containing it, as the *Recueil de Riom*. Those works and the *Vivendier* of the Kassel manuscript constitute the total of known recipe collections in French.[27] In contemporary documents there is no mention of any other such collections that may have disappeared.

Given such a limited number of recipe collections reflecting French culinary practice in the fourteenth and fifteenth centuries, and given the very brevity — relatively — of the period during which medieval cookery is recorded in the form of recipes, it is not surprising that there is a great deal of repetition in the contents of these books. Given that this *haute cuisine* is particularly that of the upper classes of French-speaking regions of continental Europe, it is understandable that recipe texts are occasionally copied fairly closely, and that "traditions" of these copies become apparent to modern scholars. Given, finally, that the nature of professional training for cooks relied upon apprenticeship to form subsequent generations of journeymen and masters, it is reasonable to expect a certain homogeneity in the French cookery of this period.

The *Vivendier* nicely illustrates the degree of uniformity and conventionality in late-medieval French cookery. Most of the dishes outlined in its recipes can be found in some form elsewhere, in at least one other collection. A few appear to have been quite popular. These are preparations that, because of the relatively late date of this collection, could be called traditional in the professional cuisine of France, as well as that of Burgundy, Savoy and the other French-speaking courts that were influenced by the taste of the royal French court. Copies of the recipes for the common dishes may be literal, suggesting that the books may have been borrowed and lent within a

---

[26] This work is also edited and studied by Carole Lambert in her *Trois réceptaires culinaires médiévaux*, particularly at pp. 134 ff.

[27] Two further collections of recipes written in Anglo-Norman, in the late-thirteenth century and between 1320 and 1340, respectively, are undoubtedly influenced to some extent by French usage; more importantly, though, they reflect the modifications of that usage in England as well as a good deal of uniquely English practice.

social or professional circle; or the copies may show minor variations due to local or contemporary taste, to faulty oral transmission, to scribal dialect or merely to error.

On the other hand, cookbooks in any age tend by their nature to grow. Any given recipe may derive from a single source or have its origin in a combination of several sources: unique invention, unwritten practice, literal copy, adaptation. The *Vivendier* seems to be a compilation from several of these sorts of sources. For some of its recipes we may suspect that we recognize the source; for others we can only speculate on the origin. The *Vivendier* affords as good an example as any of the extent to which the cookery of the early fourteenth century was accepted by the fifteenth, but was being changed as it was transmitted to kitchens in subsequent ages.

Having observed the remarkable vitality of relatively early French culinary practice, however, we should also note that this particular avatar of tradition, the *Vivendier*, is not itself known to have had a direct influence upon any other recipe collection.

(iii) Sources used for the *Vivendier*

The *Vivendier* grew by accretion over time: "newer" recipes seem to have been added in several series to "older" ones. Perhaps because of this there is little evidence that an organizing logic determined either which recipes were chosen to be copied in this collection, or the order in which they were placed in it. Only the two subsections that have explicit rubrics (*Chappitre de poissons* and *Chapittre de saulces*) leave no doubt as to the compiler's intentions. To those, with a little less certainty, we may perhaps add two further subsections: the one whose recipes each begin *Char de ...* (Recipes 9–11), and the one consisting of a sequence of various *brouets* (Recipes 20–25).

The first recipes of this compilation tend to be simple, even of a rudimentary, generic nature. In this initial part we find the traditional classics: Cameline Sauce, how to stuff eggs, Lenten Flans, Fish Cuminade, Verjuice Broth. Other than the recipes for what were termed "gross" meats — that is, joints of meat, to be roasted or boiled whole — most of the recipes are for prepared dishes that amount to pottages, mixtures of ingredients cooked in a pot; such pottages might constitute the whole dish, or else might be served upon or with another, more solid foodstuff. There are significant exceptions to this observation about the order of dishes, but in general the cooking pot plays an important role in this initial cookery of the *Vivendier*.

The recipes that follow the opening series in the compilation, for a surprisingly small number of fish and then for a few standard sauces, continue to suggest that the compiler is looking to ensure himself access to the essentials of the culinary craft. And what is particularly curious is that a good number of these recipes from the first part of the collection, apparently copied in the middle of the fifteenth century, existed

❖ I. Introduction ❖ 17

in much the same form a century and a half earlier.[28] This is, indeed, traditional French cookery. Only a few of the dishes in this first part are unusual or unknown in other French recipe collections that antedate the *Vivendier*. Almost all of the *unica* in the first part (for instance, Sicilian vermicelli, "pretend" rice, snails) are situated between Recipes 48 and 57.

Then in the history of this collection an historic event occurred: the original series of recipes was ended. A new scribal hand is evident, the spacing on the page shows more squeezing, the style of the text, and perhaps the local dialect itself, changes as well[29], and to some extent the nature of the dishes themselves is different. These additions were made firstly in order to incorporate directions for creating several quite wonderful *entremets*, and then to enrich the collection with recipes that handle singularly ordinary foodstuffs: chicken, common sea-fish and a fresh-water fish, capons, eggs, hares and chicks.

Where did these recipes come from? A quick answer must be: ultimately from a variety of sources. A full and detailed answer is virtually impossible. The same sort of variable "style" that we have remarked upon as distinguishing the second part from the first part can be seen to a lesser extent throughout the main, first part of the collection. For instance, the first 28 recipes[30] begin regularly with the phrase *Pour faire* ... , which establishes a deliberate stylistic unity. Recipes 29 and 30 are unique in that each, by means of an appended paragraph, indicates precisely the quantities of ingredients to be used. Such details were quite rare in fourteenth-century French cookery, where the author of a recipe was normally content to indicate merely the *relative* quantity of an ingredient, if this was a significant consideration at all in the dish: "much parsley, more cinnamon than the other spices, ..."[31] It is noteworthy

---

[28] See the discussion of Sources used for the *Vivendier*, below, as well as the commentary on individual recipes in the main body of the book.

[29] We may observe certain linguistic differences between the first and second parts of the *Vivendier*. Certain words and spellings change: *goust* becomes *gout*; *esve* becomes *eaue* and *yauwe*; *peu* becomes *pau* and *pauch*; the second person singular is occasionally used in this newly appended material material rather than the second person plural, regular up to Recipe 57; the introductory formula *Pour faire* ... becomes *A faire* ... ; and so forth.

[30] With the exception of Recipes 9–11, whose common beginning of *Char de* ... has its own peculiar regularity.

[31] This relative vagueness, perhaps disturbing to the ordinary modern, household cook, points to the nature of these earlier recipe collections: on the one hand, they were intended to function primarily as "memoranda" for professional cooks whose repertoire, thoroughly memorized in a long period of apprenticeship, very likely included most of the dishes copied into the principal recipe collections of the previous generation; and on the other hand, the so-called cookbooks served to document culinary practice at a

that these two recipes are copied at the end of the "general" series for prepared dishes and just before the chapter on fish. The recipes of the series 48–57, as was mentioned before, are remarkable in that they are not evidently copied from any known source.

In sum it is apparent that during its creation the collection passed through several phases and reflects several influences.

As this book was written, the writer made a selection from among recipes many, if not all, of which were already in script in other collections. That some selection went on, although not particularly carefully, is evident when the reader finds in the the copied text a reference to another recipe that was *not* itself copied. For instance, in the directions for preparing the first of the fish in the *Chapittre de poissons*, plaice (Recipe 31), the reader is instructed that it is to be cooked like a red mullet. Nowhere in the collection is this fish mentioned. Similarly, in Recipe 33 the reader never does find out just why the ray's liver is to be set aside; more than merely inexplicit, the recipe seems as though it might have been cut short, or a step in its elaboration seems for some reason to have been omitted from it.

Certain of the *Vivendier*'s recipes do indeed have counterparts in other French collections of the late Middle Ages. Primary among these is the so-called *Viandier of Taillevent*. It should be pointed out immediately, however, that the name *Viandier* is read in only two of the four extant manuscript versions of this other work, and in those versions the definite article may be explained by the apposition of the proper noun Taillevent, in the oblique case: *Cy comence le Viandier Taillevent maistre queux du Roy nostre sire* .... [32] What the scribe has written in the Kassel manuscript is *Chy commenche un vivendier et ordonnance pour apparillier pluiseurs manierez de viandes* .... As was emphasized before, this collection therefore bears a generic name: *un viandier*, "a book of victuals." The book that, for various reasons, including its very fame, became known in later times as *The Viandier* has important associations with the Kassel compilation. However, for its compiler at the time it was written, the Kassel text is still only *a viandier*. By choosing this generic term the compiler was not acknowledging any particular debt to *The Viandier* or to any

---

place during a period. This latter function is actually stated by Master Chiquart in his preamble to his *Du fait de cuisine* as he credits his lord, Duke Amédée of Savoy, for wanting him to record all that he knows about the art and science of cookery.

[32] This rubric was written at the head of the copy in the Bibliothèque Nationale manuscript; a variation of it is found in the Vatican manuscript. The earliest copy, that of the Valais manuscript roll, has suffered the abscission of the first centimetres of the parchment, which may have borne the title (if any) of the work as well as a few initial recipes. The *incipit* of the Mazarine Library copy reads, *Taillevent maistre queux du roy de France par cy enseigne a toutes gens pour apparoillier a maingier* ....

❖ I. Introduction ❖

of its early antecedents, but only fitting his book within a generally recognized type of work.

Two observations should be made when we compare our text with that of other recipe collections. In the first place, as has been already indicated, the Kassel recipes — or *their* various sources — were assembled over time in several segments; this material derived from several sources, as has been suggested. In the second place, a comparison often suggests that the links between our text and that of other collections may not have been immediate or straightforward, but rather indirect, and certain of them are obscure. Certain similarities are indeed obvious, of course.[33] However, when we see any particular parallels between texts, we should not presume that an influence must necessarily have been in one direction — that is, *from* the other version of a recipe or recipes and *upon* the version copied in the *Vivendier*. The relatively late date of the *Vivendier* is inconsequential. No matter what variant readings we may perceive, it is always possible to imagine a textual or oral history, perhaps long and complex, of any recipe such that the *Vivendier*'s version derives more closely from some *ur*-version, or even from an *oral* proto-version, than does the other version. In short, deductions about the history of recipes should always be extremely tentative.

The *incipit* in the *Vivendier* has a parallel in the *Enseignements*: *Vezci les enseingnemenz qui enseingnent a apareillier toutes manieres de viandes*. The phrasing may in fact be a conventional opening for a recipe collection, but the similarity here is still interesting.

The first nine recipes in our book are not closely related to those of any known collection. The name of Recipe 1 is, however, at least referred to in the latest copy of the *Viandier*, the Vatican version, at Recipe 163. Its quasi-occurrence in this latter work is most curious because the Vatican manuscript's scribe copied recipes for only five of the sauces announced in the Table. These five sauces are named at the very beginning of a list of fifteen sauces already copied by the scribe at the beginning of his manuscript. Then he writes the name of the *Barbe Robert*, without adding any recipe for it — and, even more curiously, without the name of this sauce having previously appeared in the Table. The *Barbe Robert* Sauce turns up in no other manuscript copy of the *Viandier*, had not been a part of the *Viandier*'s tradition as this now subsists. A recipe for it was, however, seen somewhere by

---

[33] The present editor is very reluctant to make any *ex-cathedra* declarations about sources or stemma. Given the serious gaps that remain in an adequate documentation, such conclusions must always have an intolerable element of arbitrariness about them. In Appendix B, below, he is content to provide a juxtaposition of what seem to be significant texts in the hope that readers who care to do so may draw their own conclusions — and leave lots of room for doubts.

the Vatican scribe, who was tempted to transcribe it into his collection, but whose general disinterest in sauces seems to have made him decide, after all, to ignore it. Because the *Barbe Robert* does become established in the later, printed, *Viandier* tradition, we must think that the source used by the Vatican scribe may have been one that had some connection with our collection.

A sequence of five recipes (Recipes 10–14), and another a little later (Recipe 18), are closely related to the texts read in that collection which dates from a century and a half earlier, the *Enseignements*. This surprising gap of time, from 1300 to 1450, to use very round estimates, points to one or the other of two factors, or perhaps to a combination of the two: a tradition of the *Enseignements* (as such, or these six individual recipes separately) existed and lasted over some period of time; a tradition of the *Vivendier* (as such or in part) *had* already existed over some period of time. Whatever the connection, it is clearly there.

From Recipes 19 through to 47 (with exceptions at Recipes 26, 27 and perhaps 42) our texts and those of the *Viandier* have a demonstrably close relationship. The sequence of dishes that are represented by these recipes are, firstly, pottages, then lean dishes, fish, sauces and a brief miscellany. The recipe versions in the four extant copies of the *Viandier* are not identical, though, and the version that is the "closest" to the *Vivendier* text is not always found in the same *Viandier* manuscript. If there is one *Viandier* version that resembles the *Vivendier* text most often, it is that of the Mazarine manuscript.[34] Yet the way in which the wording of our text sometimes is that of one *Viandier* manuscript, and sometimes that of another, suggests a greater complexity of both traditions than might be thought at first glance. The predominance of evidence points to a relationship (whether the influence was one way or the other) with some early version of the *Viandier*: for instance, the *Vivendier*'s Recipe 29 is for *Gellee de poisson*, while all extant copies of the *Viandier* show *Gelee de poisson . . . ou/et de char*; only the *Enseignements* resembles the *Vivendier* in considering this jelly to be for fish alone. We might be tempted to perceive, here and elsewhere, evidence that the *Vivendier* is related to a link between the *Enseignements* and the compilation that was to become the *Viandier*. A textual historian looking at written recipe collections must ask himself whether his activities are in the long run of much real use. Almost invariably he is faced with a puzzle whose missing crucial pieces leave him reduced to a lot of speculation.

Other than in the section just mentioned, no close comparison is possible with the texts of the *Viandier*. In fact, the remaining dishes for which directions are given in the *Vivendier* are for the most part remarkable for being exceptional in late-medieval French cookery.

---

[34] See, in this regard, the comment to Recipe 30, below.

❖ I. Introduction ❖

In large measure these later dishes seem to belong to a less traditional, perhaps more modern cookery. For example, the frequent use of butter in those recipes has no parallel in the *Viandier* or any other known French collection. The culinary use of snails may likewise be noted; this taste belongs neither to the *Enseignements* nor to the *Viandier* tradition as it is known. The predilection for amazing *entremets* (Recipes 58–60) further relates this section of the collection to the fifteenth century. And the prepared dishes here that bear names unknown elsewhere — *La Brehee, Pignagoscé, Rys en galles* (otherwise *Rys Contrefait*), *Vermiscaux de Cecile, Potee, Brouet de Hongherie* — emphasize that, for his material, the *Vivendier*'s compiler had access to a practice that lay beyond mainline, traditional French cookery, particularly the cookery that is represented in the *Viandier*.

Stylistically, too, the recurrent adverb *dilligamment* (in Recipes 5, 7, 30, 46, 49, 53) separates the *Vivendier* from other, and earlier, recipe collections and in a sense marks its professional independence from them. The person responsible for writing out these recipes reveals a concern that his reader understand the seriousness of a cook's work, that the dishes be properly prepared.

The scribe of the last part of the collection (from Recipe 58 onwards) was almost certainly himself the compiler of this collection at this "final" stage. He begins, for example, to copy Recipe 60, but then breaks off because he recognizes that the book already has a copy of it in Recipe 15 — in apparently much the same, if not identical, terms. Similarly, the notation *Verte folium* that is written at the end of Recipe 64 was surely appended *just as* the compiler was deciding to copy the variant preparation that Recipe 66 represents. To add a second recipe for *Potage de lievre*, at only one recipe remove from the first, must have been a conscious, deliberate decision, taken by the compiler and noted by him at the time. As he adds the second text (Recipe 66) to the collection, the writer even underscores the deliberateness of that addition by making his text parallel that of the first version of the recipe:

Recipe 64: *Prenés vo lievre et le fourboulés et lardés et le metés en rost*
. . . .
Recipe 66: *Prenés vo lievre et le lardés tresbien sans le fourboulir ne devant ne aprés, et le metés rostir* . . . .

In all probability several errors can be imputed to the scribe who was responsible for the version of the recipes found in the Kassel manuscript. In copying the ingredients for Cinnamon Broth, for instance, the scribe overlooks the cinnamon. This sort of error would not likely survive through several copies.

By way of conclusion, we can summarize thus. The *Vivendier* as it exists in the Kassel manuscript was not copied in its entirety from another source that had just those recipes in just that order. It was compiled piecemeal, perhaps over time, from several sources, on those folios that we read in the Kassel manuscript. As such in its entirety it is a unique copy of a unique compilation.

Finally, one should be very cautious about affirming that the *Vivendier* either benefitted from, or exerted, an immediate influence upon any other particular cookery manual in the late Middle Ages. In part it is probably related to a distant progenitor or off-spring of some *proto-Viandier*, but exactly how is not certain.

❖

C. The Cookery of the *Vivendier*

(i) The kitchen and its utensils

The recipes of the *Vivendier* do not refer extensively to either the kitchen, its facilities or its furnishings. Virtually everything that is in the kitchen has to be inferred from the processes that are mentioned as each dish is to be elaborated from its recipe. In virtually every instance, these physical elements are ones that would be considered entirely common in any fifteenth-century French (or probably European) kitchen.

In all likelihood the compiler of the *Vivendier* foresaw the need for only an open fire in order to cook the dishes for which he assembled the recipes. The fuel of this fire is perhaps assumed to be coal, rather than wood (Recipe 16; in Recipe 15 the fire must be regulated evenly along the length of a fish); there is no concern about smoke contaminating the flavour of whatever is exposed to a wood fire, as is occasionally expressed in recipes that were written earlier (*Viandier*, Recipe 45, Mazarine manuscript; Chiquart, Recipe 73). The fire must burn between andirons which will hold spits for roasting. Beside and over it, a trammell likely projected, perhaps on a swivelling bracket, to hold pots in order to boil liquids; certain recipes direct that the pot is to be drawn back from the fire, this action most normally being accomplished merely by swinging the pivoting arm (Recipes 30, 44). A grill or gridiron is expressly called for in order to toast bread over this fire, or over open coals (Recipe 6; see also Recipes 4 and 64 where bread is to be burnt), and we may suppose that a similar grill is used for roasting the middle third of the three-way fish (Recipe 15), and also perhaps for holding pans (as in Recipes 26, 62, 66). A baking oven is expressly required only once (Recipe 66), although its presence in or near the kitchen is implicit for the baking of other dishes.

Both a heavy and a slender spit are needed in this kitchen, for roasting meat (Recipes 10, 59) and an eel (Recipe 43); and the presence of a skewer is implied when it is used to bleed a lamprey (Recipe 43).

A pan, called a *payelle*, is used to boil liquid ingredients (Recipes 26, 62, 66); this must be of relatively small dimensions because it is optionally of either iron or earthenware (Recipe 66). Another variety of pan in use is a dripping pan (Recipe 58), used to collect the juices of a roasting meat. A pot is mentioned in several recipes (5, 15, 28, 64), although never with any indication of the material of which it is made. In one instance a pot has a lid (Recipe 42). A curious insistence is also found (Recipes 30, 46) that the pot be "new" and not merely "clean"; this specification likely indicates that the normal cooking pot might be thought to be of pottery and cheaply replaced when it had become encrusted with the vestiges of former preparations.

Among its utensils the kitchen has a *louce* (normally in Francian *louche*), or large spoon (Recipe 30; Recipe 66 uses this spoon as a measure, a *louchiee*). Such stirring spoons are employed to keep a semi-liquid mixture from burning (Recipe 5). There is a spatula to turn an omelet, for the same purpose (Recipe 7). There is evidence of a basting spoon (Recipes 10, 66). A skimmer is used to remove the scum from the surface of a boiling mixture (Recipes 5, 9 and, potentially, 42). A variety of knives is on hand for cutting ingredients; the verb *hachier* recurs in a number of recipes (3, 5, 7, 8, 22, 45, 49, 62), indicating the presence, and regular use, of a cleaver.

A grater must be available to reduce bread and toast to crumbs (for example in Recipe 53), as well as cheese (Recipe 7). A filter or sieve (called the *estamine*) is in constant use for reducing ingredients such as ground, macerated spices and moist breadcrumbs to even finer particles; this filter is usually a coarsely woven fabric which is washed clean between uses. A more tightly woven fabric is also present in the *Vivendier*'s kitchen and serves to hold a foodstuff cleanly (27, 44), sometimes while it drains (Recipe 29, 57). A piece of cloth, called "linen", is likewise at hand to wrap around the tail third of the three-way fish (Recipe 15).

A quite peculiar substance is referred to in the *Vivendier*, and that is *le bel sablon*. The context, and particularly the definite article, suggest that this "bed of sand" was commonly available to a cook and served to hold a hot cooking pot and to absorb its heat slowly, or to allow this heat to dissipate slowly (Recipe 29).

Certain tableware also appears among these recipes, although not properly or directly related to the culinary activities of the kitchen. *Escuelles, plats, hanaps* and *pots* (these last in Recipe 58) are primarily serving vessels. They would be of metal (likely pewter, perhaps silver) or of wood, and would be available on the serving dresser in the kitchen.

(ii) Ingredients

The dishes described in the recipes of the *Vivendier* make use of a limited number of ingredients. Some of these foodstuffs were commonly consumed throughout France in the fifteenth century; others are worth noting as peculiar to this collection, either in the exceptional frequency that the substance appears in these recipes, or in the exceptional appearance of the foodstuff in itself. To the first category we may usefully add a contrary classification: foodstuffs that are relatively common in other recipe collections but are ignored by the *Vivendier*.[35]

---

[35] For an overview of the ingredients that are named among the recipes of the *Vivendier*, see

❖ I. Introduction ❖ 25

Of frequent use here is sugar; fourteen of the 66 recipes contain it either as an ingredient or as a garnish. This fondness for sweetness is characteristic of the century and may be seen in other collections from the time. As has already been noted, sea-fish seem to enjoy as much favour as fresh-water fish. Eel appears in four recipes, a surprising frequency; carp turns up in three — to which can be added the two recipes for tench, a fish that resembles carp. Egg yolks (alone) enter into thirteen of the prepared dishes.

Adding to the particularly rich nature of this cookery, dairy products enjoy somewhat more prominence than in any other recipe collection, whether from France or another region. We find here not only cow's milk in three dishes (Recipes 30, 41, 46), although it is rare in even larger recipe books, but cream in another three (Recipes 7, 8, 17). Butter, likewise rare in other collections, is called for in an amazing eleven recipes and cheese in eight.[36]

The flavour of onions[37] and garlic seems to be enjoyed by our compiler, with a total of ten recipes incorporating one or the other of these. And in three instances mustard is called upon to lend its distinctive taste to a dish; the initial recipe in our collection is essentially a mustard sauce. By the fifteenth century the use of mustard had become relatively infrequent in French cookery; its appearance in the *Vivendier* may have some cultural significance. The late-fourteenth-century Champenois poet Eustache Deschamps (*c.* 1340–*c.* 1406) rails against the ubiquitous prevalence of mustard in Germanic cookery, and for that reason abhors having to travel in German territory. It seems that our compiler does not share Deschamps's dislike of this condiment.

A second category in an analysis of the ingredients in these recipes, is negative: those that are in common use elsewhere but not here. Compared with other collections, fish play a comparatively minor role here; in the *Viandier* itself, some 60 of the 170 recipes in the "classical" version are devoted to fish, even though most of these recipes are relatively brief. That number is roughly 35% of the total recipes in that large collection, as compared with some 25% in the present collection, and more than 50% in the case of the *Du fait de cuisine* of Chiquart. Our collection has no use for egg whites; where the whites are distinguished from the yolks (in

---

the listing in Part A: Ingredients in the Recipes, of Section III: Ingredients and Glossary, below.

[36] In the advice entitled *Contre pestilence* that follows the *Vivendier* in the Kassel manuscript, Dr. Jacques Despars counsels against the consumption of *laitages* in times of plague, as if dairy products might be recognized as a distinct and significant category of foodstuff by the manuscript's reader.

[37] This despite the fact that there is only one dish based generically upon onions as the essential ingredient, a *civé* (Recipe 27).

Recipe 62, for instance), this is particularly in order to separate the yolk to prepare it alone for eating. Furthermore, whole eggs — that is, both yolks and eggs together — appear in only three instances (Recipe 3, 7, 8 and 63). Eggs are important, as was noted above, primarily for their yolks. Among the meats, not much venison is consumed — in fact, no large game animals are mentioned. Only generically and vaguely is "venison" referred to (Recipes 4, 11). The only game identified is what traditionally was classified as small game — whether its actual provenance was domestic or wild for the kitchens of the well-to-do: rabbit (Recipe 22) and hare (Recipes 64, 66). There are no specific game birds here, a source of meat much exploited by the *Viandier* and other recipe books; even the generic *oysiaux* (Recipes 58, 59, 66) occurs as a supplementary variant in recipes for poultry or small game animals. There are no mollusks and only one crustacean (Recipe 42).

Herbs are handled in this kitchen, in at least the variety if not quite the frequency that they appear in other collections: here we find chervil, cress, hyssop, laserwort, lavender, laurel, parsley, pennyroyal, sage, sorrel — with parsley far and away the most popularly used. Of the spices, galingale (or galangal) and long pepper are rare in French cookery of the time but relatively better known by English cooks. Among our recipes fresh grape juice, or must, is not listed as an ingredient at all. In other collections must is well enough known that the cooks using those recipes are expected to have a supply of it on hand.

A final category is of those foodstuffs that are used here but are not common elsewhere. In this respect we would have to draw attention again to the *laitages* — cow's milk, cream and, especially, butter — mentioned earlier. The dressing of snails for consumption is read in only two other manuscript locations: the *Menagier de Paris* and the Italian *Neapolitan Collection*.[38] Among incidental ingredients we may observe the unusual specification of "brown sugar" (Recipe 64) and rosewater (Recipe 52). Although the taste for pepper (along with mustard) had waned in the fifteenth century, it is still required for three recipes here (Recipes 30, 40, 55); even more strangely, long pepper seems to have tweaked the compiler's taste buds with its completely exceptional use in no fewer than seven dishes. And finally, the naming of goose grease (Recipe 66, for basting hare) is unique among the French recipes of the time. The flesh of a goose or gosling is not handled anywhere in our recipes; however, its preparation — particularly by roasting — constituted a recognized and distinct activity among the commercial food trades.

---

[38] See the editorial comment to Recipe 57, below.

(iii) Other observations

The cookery of this group of recipes has several particularities.

Although frying occurs in 21 of these 66 recipes in the *Vivendier*, the frying medium is specifically oil — that is, olive oil — in only three of these cases.[39] In other cases the liquid used for frying is roughly evenly divided between melted lard and melted butter. Three terms refer to frying: *frire, refrire* and *suffrire*. Of the three, the last is the most used in these recipes, with a surprising 14 occurrences against six for the simple *frire*. The sense of the verb *suffrire* is "to fry lightly, partially," "to brown or sear" or "to sautee".[40] Its predominance here points up an habitual procedure in preparing dishes, particularly those involving meat: a large number of the preparations (for instance, in Recipe 52) require the cook to begin by sauteing the foodstuff, and then to put it into a liquid mixture in order to boil it and, usually, to add flavour and exert a corrective tempering. Technically, we may observe today that this brief frying should offer the benefit of sealing the natural juices of the meat (or whatever foodstuff) within it before it undergoes its primary cooking.

A similar observation should be made concerning the verb *fourboulir* (Recipes 64, 66). Such a parboiling had become part of a compound strategy for cooking a meat. Again, it resulted from the cook's willingness to adopt more complex procedures in order to make his principal foodstuff more gastronomically appealing to his patron.

The verb *remuer* is without exception accompanied in our texts by the adverb *dilligamment*. We find it also modifying *retourner* in the delicate operation of flipping an omelet (Recipe 7). This adverb is remarkably strong. The author/compiler seems concerned that the cook identify the really crucial moments of his professional work, in order to be prepared to exercise particular attention and care at those times.

One notable peculiarity of the *Vivendier* is that this collection contains no recipe for a *blanc manger*. This almond, rice and chicken dish was a *sine qua non* of latemedieval recipe collections and meals. We may wonder whether the compiler felt that, gastronomically, the dish had become somewhat *passé*.

❖

---

[39] Recipes 13, 15 and 32. Recipe 60 repeats the beginning of Recipe 15, where the title includes the mention of frying one-third of the fish in oil. In one of the three, Recipe 15, an alternative to this oil is allowed: butter.

[40] See the comment to Recipe 8.

D. Editorial principles

This edition of the *Vivendier* is conservative. It aims to offer the manuscript text as accurately as possible. Emendations are few, and are presented only when the scribe's text, through his own fault or otherwise, is clearly in error, and only accompanied, in a footnote, with a clear statement of what has been changed. The modern English translation is for the benefit of those who lack facility in fifteenth-century French. In a few cases the translation implicitly proposes an interpretation of the sense of the text.

The comments that follow each recipe are often rather hesitant in nature. Much information can occasionally be given about a particular recipe; even more can be speculated. The editor has tried to be reasonably brief so as not to bore the expert, yet still be helpful to the interested novice. Obviously, as the comments indicate here and there, a few intractable mysteries remain in this text as in other similar ones: both experts and novices still have much to learn about late-medieval cookery.

The edition has collected the recipes' vocabulary in a Glossary, partly in order to facilitate scholarly study of this terminology. Just previous to the Glossary proper the interested reader will see a simple listing of the culinary ingredients, the foodstuffs, that are used in this cookery. It will be recognized that the categories into which the foodstuffs are sorted in this listing are to some degree artificial.

The Appendices are intended to facilitate the work of scholars who may wish to pursue the question of the sources used by the compiler of this particular assortment of recipes. Throughout this edition the editor makes certain observations on the matter of sources. Such observations are meant always to be tentative. Individual recipes may be borrowed or lent in a written form quite independent of what may be part of a "book". Cooks may also "learn" recipes and so quite literally "possess" them; indeed, given the oral nature of late-medieval professional apprenticeship, written transmission of recipes was in principle superfluous. We may reasonably guess that it was only at some relatively advanced phase in his professional career that a cook decided, or was persuaded, to commit that oral text to writing; yet at that stage in his career many influences, and certainly not the least of these his own experience, have likely contributed to the formation of such a learned, practical technician as a cook. Furthermore, when, as in the *Vivendier*, we are dealing with a written text whose intent is primarily compilatory and whose author is probably at one remove from the practical work of the kitchen, the picture of "sources" is all the less distinct.

With the current general lack of solid evidence in this matter, questions of textual sources and culinary influence here and elsewhere are safest left in the realm of very hesitant conjecture. The editor feels that generally it would be foolhardy to go much beyond such conjecture. We repeat that Appendix B, which juxtaposes similar recipe versions, may help an interested reader to speculate in one direction or another.

The Bibliography of Appendix D is indeed summary. It is intended merely to be an initial resource for anyone who may wish to investigate further either the nature of French cookery in the late Middle Ages in general or, by comparison, cookery in the *Vivendier* in particular.

❖

II. The *Vivendier*

Original Text with Translation and Commentary* on the Recipes and Cookery

(Kassel, Gesamthochschul-Bibliothek Kassel, 4° Ms. med. 1, ff. 154r–164v)

[f. 154r] **Chy commenche un vivendier et ordonnance[†] pour aparillier pluiseurs manierez de viandes.**

Here begins a cookery book and directions for preparing numerous sorts of dishes.

❖ ❖ ❖ ❖ ❖ ❖ ❖ ❖

[1. Barbe Robert]

Et premiers, pour faire une barbe Robert: prenez un poy de belle esve, et le mettez boullir avoec du bure; et puis y mettez du vin, de le moustarde et du vergus et des espices teles et si fortez que vous y arez vo[1.1] goust, et laissiez tout bien boullir ensamble; puis prenez vostre poulet par pieces et le mettez dedens et laissiez boullir une onde seullement, puis si le rostez; et gardez qu'il y ait brouet par raison; et qui soit un poy couloure de saffren.

Firstly, to make a Barbe Robert. Get a little clear water and set it to boil with some butter; then add in wine, mustard, verjuice and such spices and as strong as you like, and let everything boil together. Then get your pieces of chicken, put them in and let them boil only briefly; then roast them. Watch that there is a reasonable amount of broth. It should be coloured a little with saffron.

The *Barbe Robert* is essentially a "fortified" mustard sauce — that is, a boiled mustard with additional spicing.

As Recipe 163, the Vatican copy of the *Viandier* shows only the name of this sauce: *La barbe Robert, autrement appelee la Taillemaslee*. No recipe is

---

* In the following comments, references to early French recipe collections and editions are more completely set out in the Bibliography of Appendix D, below.
† ms.: *ordonn*, with a long nasal superscript.
[1.1] ms.: *sic* here and in Recipes 64 and 66 — which are versions of the same recipe — with no abbreviation sign. Elsewhere *vostre* is written some 40 times either in full or vre with a superscript slur (as in *prenez vostre poulet* immediately below).

offered there. In a sixteenth-century printed cookbook that is rooted in the *Viandier* tradition[1.2], we find a recipe for *Saulce barbe Robert* which is at least related to our text — the name suggests that. However, apart from being a spicey, hot mustard mixture, it has clearly been modified rather freely over the intervening generations. We may note in the *Vivendier*, though, that the direction to use *des espices teles et si fortez que vous y avez vo goust*, seems to give the cook considerable latitude in elaborating this sauce. The later, printed version additionally includes fried onions and vinegar; and, rather than a cooking sauce for chicken, it is to be used to dress roast rabbit or fried fish. At least the sauce's name appears to have been durable.

❖ ❖ ❖ ❖ ❖ ❖ ❖ ❖

[2. Assisse d'anguillez]

Pour faire assisse d'anguillez : mettez les pourboulir ainsi qu'a moitié, puis les tirez hors a part ; prenez pain blancq tempré en la dicte[2.1] esve, et passé parmy l'estamine ; saffren pour donner couleur, gingembre, canelle et graine, deffait de vin aigre[2.2] ; faictez tout boullir bien ensemble ; sel et vergus pour agouster ; puis remettez vos anguilles parcuire dedens sans despechier ; et dreschiez chaudement.

To make a Serving of Eels. Set them to parboil to about half-done, then take them out and set them aside. Get white bread tempered in that broth and put it through the strainer; saffron for colour, ginger, cinnamon and grains of paradise tempered in vinegar; boil everything together well; salt and verjuice for flavour. Then put your eels back in to cook slowly. Dish it up hot.

The sequence of three operations found in this preparation is common: a meat is half-cooked, a cooking sauce is elaborated and brought to a boil, the cooking of the meat is finished in this sauce. Though the recipe here is not explicit, the cooking sauce likely functioned as a serving sauce as well, either being poured

---

[1.2] *Fleur de toute cuisine*, Paris (Pierre Pidoux), 1548, f° 45v. This recipe is reproduced in the editor's publication of the *The Viandier of Taillevent*, p. 226. A similar version of the Barbe Robert appears in the *Grand cuisinier de toute cuisine*, Douai (Jean Bogart), 1583; this is reproduced in Pichon and Vicaire's edition of *Le Viandier de Guillaume Tirel dit Taillevent*, Paris (Techener), 1892, p. 109.

[2.1] Here and regularly in the text this word is abbreviated by means of *dce* with a superscript slur. Many of the more common words are similarly abbreviated by means of such a superscript: *faictez, vostre, prenez, bien*, etc.

[2.2] Regularly so written as two distinct words in the manuscript. Only in Recipes 36, 37, 39, 61, 63 and 66 is the space between the *n* and the *a* so reduced as to suggest that the scribe might have considered he was writing a single word.

as a garnish over the whole eels or, less probably in the case of this dish, being presented to the table in bowls in order for diners to dip cut pieces of eel into it.

❖ ❖ ❖ ❖ ❖ ❖ ❖ ❖

[3. Chaudel sur eulx pochiez]

Pour faire un chaudel sur eulx pochiez: prenez persin hachié menu et refrit en bure, esve et vergus, faictez boulir ensamble; mettez vos soupes en plas, et oes et vostre brouet par dessus.

To make a Caudel on Poached Eggs. Get finely chopped parsley — that has been sauteed in butter — water and verjuice, and boil these together. Set out your sops on platters, then your eggs, and your broth over top.

Though this recipe is for what is called a caudle, its name might also have designated the dish for which the caudle is made. Properly, this is a sort of sop, a dish whose base is a slice or chunk of bread.

Many sorts of caudle are recognized in late-medieval recipes. The term derives from the Latin *calidum* and *caldellum*, "hot". In the suffix, the normal phonetic changes of standard French may, perhaps confusingly, have suggested the French word for "water"; occasionally the name *chaudeau* is found. The preparation is, in fact, generically a hot, runny composition or beverage. Traditionally the caudle was composed as a sickdish: quite appropriately the *Viandier*'s Flemish Caudle was copied among other sickdishes. The *Viandier*'s Caudle is composed merely of egg yolks beaten into boiling water, along with optional verjuice.

The frying of parsley in oil, before it enters into a mixture (see this also in Recipe 21, below), is rarely seen in earlier recipe collections, but does become a relatively common procedure in French cookery of the next two centuries. It is frequent, for instance, in the recipes of La Varenne; in a surprising range of significant respects the practice of this seventeenth-century worthy remains that of the end of the Middle Ages.

❖ ❖ ❖ ❖ ❖ ❖ ❖ ❖

[4. Assisse de venoison]

[f. 154v] Pour faire assisse de venoison: mettez le char boullir en vin, et quant elle sera bien cuite, si prenez brun pain bien rosti noir et tempré en vin, passé parmy l'estamine, saffren, gingembre, canelle et graine, destempré de vin aigre; faictez tout boulir ensamble; qu'il soit bien brun au dreschier.[4]

---

[4] ms.: *dreschr* with a superscript *i*.

To make a Serving of Venison. Set the meat to boil in wine. When it is well cooked, get burnt toast of brown bread, tempered in wine and put through the strainer; saffron, ginger, cinnamon and grains of paradise, [ground and] distempered with vinegar; let everything boil together. It should be quite brown when dished up.

This recipe is generic in nature: it is for a presentation sauce that is suitable for a serving of any sort of venison. The recipe's name, with the term *assisse* (used also with regard to the eels of Recipe 2), indicates that it is this sauce that in fact "makes" or distinguishes a serving of venison.

❖ ❖ ❖ ❖ ❖ ❖ ❖ ❖

[5. Pasté en pot]

Pour faire un pasté en pot[5.1] **: prenez tel char que vouldrez hachié bien menu, et le mettez bien cuire dedens un pot; vin, esve grasse assez, sel egalment et espices, et soit bien escumé tout premierement; puis prenez vos espices, pain froyé ou passé, et moyeulx d'oes bien batus, saffren un poy pour donner couleur; faictez boullir a poy d'esve grasse largement et bien couvert qu'il puist bien estuver, en remuant dilligamment qu'il n'arde.**

To make a Pasty in a Pot. Get whatever meat you like, chopped up finely, and set it to cook in a pot with wine, good greasy bouillon, a judicious amount of salt, and spices; this should first be skimmed. Then get your spices, ground or sieved bread, well beaten egg yolks and a little saffron for colour; boil it in just enough (?) good greasy bouillon, and covered tightly, for it to stew, and stirring carefully so that it doesn't burn.

Un pasté seems at first glance to be a generic misnomer for this dish, since the masculine word normally designates a "pasty" or "pie" (of pastry). The term is used in Recipes 13 and 14 where it applies to a preparation consisting of a pastry shell and its filling — even though there is no explicit direction in those recipes (or in Recipe 12) that the cook is to prepare a pie or turnover shell. In the present recipe, *un pasté* designates, literally, a dish of meat which has been reduced to a "paste." Such continues to be the case of the modern *pâté en terrine* or *pâté en pot*[5.2] — the latter of which phrases is, indeed, exactly the name of our dish here.

❖ ❖ ❖ ❖ ❖ ❖ ❖ ❖

[5.1] ms.: *pos* changed to *pot*.

[5.2] As distinct, for instance, from a *pâté en croûte*.

[6. Saulse cameline]

Pour faire une saulse cameline : prenez pain blancq harlé sur le greil, sy le mettez temprer en vin rouge et vin aigre, passé parmy l'estamine, canelle assez, et gingembre, clou, graine, macis, poivre long et saffren un poy et sel ; faictez boullir ou non boullir comme vouldrez ; aucun y mettent du chucquere.

To make a Cameline Sauce. Get white bread toasted on the grill, set it to temper in red wine and vinegar, and strain it, along with a good deal of cinnamon, and ginger, cloves, grains of paradise, mace, long pepper and a little saffron. Finish it off either boiled or not as you like. Some people put sugar in it.

Cameline Sauce is a brownish mixture (the colour of a camel, after which it is named) whose principal ingredient is cinnamon. Here the primacy of the cinnamon is marked by the word *assez*; some writers even mistakenly show the sauce's name as *cannelline*. The *Viandier* classifies this as an unboiled sauce — that is, a cold sauce — although our text allows it to be prepared either hot or cold.

The presence of sugar in the ingredients list, even though optional, tends to make a reader think of a relatively late version of this staple sauce.

❖ ❖ ❖ ❖ ❖ ❖ ❖ ❖

[7. Votte lombarde]

[f. 155r (cxli)] Pour faire une votte lombarde : prenés oes frais, fin fromage fondant, gratté ou hachié menu ou par dez quarez, cresme douce et vin, canelle et chucquere ; batez tout ensamble ; puis ayez bure fres fondu chault, mettez dedens en retournant dilligamment qu'il n'arde.

To make a Votte Lombarde. Get fresh eggs, fine runny cheese, grated or chopped finely or cut into cubes, with fresh cream and wine, cinnamon and sugar; beat everything together. Then get hot melted fresh butter and put this in it, stirring attentively so it doesn't burn.

The use of a soft, runny cheese, fresh cream and fresh butter seems to suggest an origin for this recipe that is closer to the scribe's homeland in north-eastern France rather than to foreign parts, even Lombardy.

The generic dish *votte* is not commonly represented in late-medieval recipe collections. Godefroy (Vol. 8, p. 299c) recognizes the terms *vote* and *votte* as variant forms for *volte*, and glosses all of the words with the sense of "omelette, crêpe". For the entry he provides an illustration from Archives of Tournai — the region of our manuscript — in 1356.[7.1] As for the qualification, we may note that "Lombard" occurs in the name of an English custard dish called *Crustade Lumbard*.[7.2]

The recipe's insistence upon a constant stirring might produce a sort of sweet, creamy scrambled eggs with a cinnamon flavour. As is occasionally the case, our author remains silent on the manner of serving this preparation.

❖ ❖ ❖ ❖ ❖ ❖ ❖ ❖

[8. Pour farsir oes]

Pour farsir oes: soient cuis en l'escaille tout durs, et puis pellez, et hostez les mioefz; puis prenez persin, cresme, fin fromage fondant com[8.1] **dessus, et les mioefz, tout hachié bien menu et broyé, pourldre**[8.2] **de duc ou canelle et chucquere; remplissiez vos blans d'oes comme devant; les serrez bien d'un filet que la farse ne chiee, puis les suffrisiez en beau bure fres bien chaut; et les enfarinez se voulez, et dorez.**

To Stuff Eggs. Hard boil them in their shells, then shell them and remove their yolks. Then get parsley, cream, fine runny cheese as in the previous recipe, and the yolks, with everything chopped up finely; add in ground Poudre de Duc *or cinnamon and sugar. Fill up your egg whites again. Wrap them carefully in a net so the stuffing doesn't fall out; then brown them in good hot fresh butter, and coat them with flour if you wish.*

The practice of stuffing eggs — here with a rich mixture of cream and soft cheese, mixed with the hard yolks, spiced and sweetened — is not as common

---

[7.1] This word, and the dish, may be related to the low-German word *vlot*, meaning "soft" or "creamy," as in *vlotkese*. See the *Mittelniederdeutsches Kochbuch*, ed. Hans Wiswe, "Nachlese zum ältesten mittelniederdeutschen Kochbuch," *Braunschweigisches Jahrbuch*, 39 (1958), p. 51.

[7.2] Recipe 17 in the first of the *Two Fifteenth-Century Cookery-Books* ed. by Thomas Austin for the Early English Text Society, Original Series, 91, London (Oxford University Press), 1888 (repr. 1964), p. 51. This "custard" is again called *Crustad Lumbard* in the *Ordinance of Pottage*, ed. Constance Hieatt, London (Prospect Books), 1988; Recipe 123. Though these recipes combine eggs and cream, both lack cheese but include ingredients, such as dates and marrow, that lend a different character to the dish; both are made in a pastry shell like a quiche. The last collection also contains "lombard fritters" (*freture lumbard*, Recipe 109) which bear a slight similarity to our dish.

[8.1] ms.: An indistinct pair of light pen strokes, sketching a spiral whose tail is not clear, could be an abbreviation for *con* or *com*. The reference would be to the use of such creamy cheese in the previous recipe.

[8.2] ms.: *sic*.

in early French cookery as in Italian recipes of the fifteenth century. See, for instance, the *Ova piene* in Maestro Martino's *Libro de arte coquinaria*.[8.3]

The ground spice mixture known as *Poudre de Duc* was well known among cooks.[8.4] The *Menagier de Paris* (Recipe 317) directs his reader on the making of hypocras (with fine powdered cinnamon, ginger, grains of paradise, nutmeg and galingale — the major late-medieval culinary spices *less* pepper), and then appends a *nota* that *la pouldre et le succre meslez ensemble font pouldre de duc*. At the beginning of the seventeenth century still, though doubtless referring to late-sixteenth-century usage, Randle Cotgrave glosses this compound as, "a powder made of Sugar and Cinnamon, & having (sometimes) other Aromaticall simples added unto them." We may note that our text offers the alternative of *poudre de duc* or cinnamon and sugar.

The verb *suffrire* makes its first appearance in the collection here. It will recur frequently whenever the cook wishes a foodstuff to undergo a relatively light frying. For the Stuffed Eggs, this frying is intended merely to heat and brown them; with meats the treatment often forms the initial step in a two- or three-phase procedure and is preliminary to a subsequent cooking.

❖   ❖   ❖   ❖   ❖   ❖   ❖   ❖

[9. Char de porc fresche]

Char de porc fresche soit mise temprer en belle esve une demie heure, et toutes aultres chars affin que la char soit plus blanche quant elle

---

[8.3] Ed. Emilio Faccioli, *Arte della cucina*, 2 vols., Milano (Il Polifilo), 1966; Vol. I, pp. 180–81.

[8.4] The author of the *Libre de sent soví* describes the making of *Polvora de duch fina* in Recipe 220. *Per una liura: Primerament tu pendras: una liura de sucre blanch; canella, mige hunsa que sia fina; gingebre que sia bo, un quart e mig; giroffle, nous noscades, garangal, cardemoni, entre tot un quart. E tot aso picaras, e pessar-ho as per sadas*. This is, therefore, a mixture of sugar, cinnamon, ginger, cloves, nutmeg, galingale and cardamom. Similarly the *Libre del coch* of Mestre Robert offers two recipes for *Polvora de duch* (Recipes 29 and 30) in which the ingredients are cinnamon, ginger, cloves and sugar in one case and ginger, galingale, cinnamon, long pepper, nutmeg, grains of paradise and sugar in the other. See Barbara Santich's comments on this mixture in her article "L'influence italienne sur l'évolution de la cuisine médiévale catalane," *Manger et boire au moyen âge*, 2 vols., Paris (Les Belles Lettres), 1984; Vol. II, p. 135. She proposes that the qualification *duch* derives either from the phrase that identified a mixture of the most commonly used spices, *specie dolce* in Italian, or "mild spices"; or else from the fact that this mixture of common spices was made *doux* with the addition of sugar.

sera cuitte; soit cuitte en esve et bien escumee[9]; puis ayez pain passé, persin, sailles et autrez herbes, saffren et vergus; faictez tout boullir ensamble.

Fresh Pork. Set it to temper in pure water for a half hour, and likewise any other meat so that the meat will be whiter. When it is done, it should be cooked in water and skimmed carefully. Then get sieved bread, parsley, sage and other herbs, saffron and verjuice; boil everything together.

The recipe for newly slaughtered pork (as opposed to the salted meat) begins a series of three directions for handling the meats of a small variety of animals. The generalization that the author has put near the beginning of this recipe, ... *et toutes aultres chars*, helps to lend a universal sense to this recipe. The common character of the proper handling of such meats is confirmed in the next recipe.

The initial treatment of blanching a foodstuff preliminary to cooking it is relatively commonplace. In the next recipe the verb *rafreschir* will designate this operation. Later generations of cooks will use the verb *blanchir* for it, although in large measure what it accomplishes is a plumping of the meat or vegetable.

Remarkably, the pork is cooked by boiling. Such is not the usual treatment of this meat — reputed, as it is, to be exceptionally moist in nature. We should note, though, that the recipe calls for the adjunction of a range of herbs whose generally warm and dry natures may be counted upon to effect the necessary correction of temperament. These herbs are mixed with saffron to produce a hue that medieval French cooks regularly called *vert gay* — that is, gaudy green or, literally, cheery green. For another instance of this colour see Recipe 25, below.

❖ ❖ ❖ ❖ ❖ ❖ ❖ ❖

[10. Char de mouton]

[f. 155v] **Char de mouton soit mis rafreschir pareillement pour estre la char plus blanche, puis mis rostir en la broche, et lardé de persin et de sauge quant elle sera my cuitte, et arosee de vin aigre ou de vergus en rostissant; ou soit mis boullir en esve avoec persin, ysope, saille, polioel et autrez bonnes herbes; et mengié a la sauce vert ou au vergus renouvellé. Le pouldré[10.1] a la moustarde.**

Mutton should likewise be set to "freshen" so the meat will be whiter; then it is set to roast on a spit. When it is half cooked, it is larded with parsley and sage; as it

---

[9] ms: *escumet.*

[10.1] In all likelihood this *pouldré* is a scribal error for *salé:* see the commentary.

roasts, it is basted with vinegar or verjuice. Alternatively, it should be set to boil in water with parsley, hyssop, sage, pennyroyal and other good herbs. It should be eaten with Green Sauce or with renewed verjuice. [Salted mutton is eaten] with mustard.

Unlike the pork of the previous recipe, mutton may undergo either a roasting or a boiling. In either case the extensive use of a variety of herbs remains central in the treatment of this meat as well. Even the first of the serving sauces, Green Sauce, is based on the herb parsley.

The so-called "renewed verjuice", *verjus renouvellé*, likely refers to a stock of verjuice whose tang has been restored by the adjunction of newly pressed verjuice. For boiled mutton, the Mazarine manuscript of the *Viandier* (Recipe 3) allows as an option a serving sauce of *verjus reverdi*.[10.2] Elsewhere, the *Viandier* mentions *verjus vert*, the sense of the qualification alluding to its colour, green, rather than to any state or freshness or tangy taste. This is indeed an option for dressing roast mutton in the *Viandier*'s Recipe 34 (Mazarine manuscript): ... *au verjus vert*. The adjective *renouvellé* in our text doubtless recognizes that verjuice by its nature was at its best only for a limited time after it was produced in the middle of the summer; by the following summer it had lost the acidic bite which made it such a valued ingredient in cookery.

The extensive use of herbs in this recipe's alternative treatment of mutton is exceptional. As a matter of curious coincidence it may be pointed out that earlier in the manuscript containing the *Vivendier* the compiler has placed a copy of Chapter 16 of the *Herbal* of pseudo Macer Floridus[10.3]; the excerpt begins with an analysis of the herb pennyroyal: *Polieul est caud et secs ou tierch degree selonc que dient les philozophes. Cheste herbe deffendés as femmes gras, car se elles en usoient souvent lez fruyt seroit avortin. Item se les femme buvoient de la dite herbe avoecq vin tievene, elle fait issir les fleurs.* .... In the article on "Pennyroyal *Mentha pulegium*" in the *Random House Book of Herbs* (New York, 1990), the authors, Rober Phillips and Nicky Foy write, " ... This plant should not be used medicinally as, according to Weiss, pulegon, the main constituent of the volatile oil, is very toxic and can cause abortion" (p. 34). The same herb is again included further on, in Recipe 45.

The occurrence here of two terms to designate the herb sage may be noted: firstly *sauge*, and then the dialectal *saille(s)*, which the scribe has already used in

---

[10.2] See the section of juxtaposed texts in Appendix A, below.

[10.3] *De viribus seu de virtutibus herbarum*, probably written by Othon de Meudon before 1161. The enduring popularity of this work, and its influence, are attested by such copies as in the Kassel manuscript, even well on into the fifteenth century.

the preceding recipe.

The final phrase of this recipe presents a problem. We may read that the boiled mutton is sauced and then "sprinkled with mustard sauce" — a sort of double saucing, which is not at all usual. In this case *pouldré* might well be an imperative, with the *z* left off: a similar form is found in Recipe 15, *le coulouré*. A much more probable understanding of the word *pouldré* is that we have here a scribal error for some such word as *salé, rosti, lardé, boulli* or even (again) *mengié*. The conclusion of Recipe 3 in the *Viandier* specifies mustard sauce for boiled *salted* meats (including mutton); the *Vivendier*'s next recipe, Recipe 11 for venison, below, has exactly this phrase in the same final location: *le salé a la mostarde*. In Appendix A, below, we may see that the corresponding directions in the *Enseignements* ends with just this same phrase: *Por char de mouton. ... E mengié a la sause verte; la salee a la moustarde* (Recipe 12; ll. 39–40). We would argue for the word *salé* at this point in our text as well.

❖ ❖ ❖ ❖ ❖ ❖ ❖ ❖

[11. Char de venoison]

Char de venoison soit cuitte en vin et en esve, et mengié au poivre chault; le salé a la mostarde.

Venison should be cooked in wine and water; it is eaten with Hot Pepper Sauce; salted venison [is eaten] with mustard.

This recipe for Venison is substantially what is read in the *Viandier*. A recipe for the Hot Pepper Sauce will be provided later: *Poivre chault noir* (Recipe 40, below).

❖ ❖ ❖ ❖ ❖ ❖ ❖ ❖

[12. Flans de quaresme]

Pour faire flans de quaresme: cuissez anguillez a mort, puis hostés les arrestez et tout le noir, puis le broyez en un mortier; gingembre, graine et saffren, deffait de lait d'agmandes ou poy de fleur[12.1] d'amidun ou de ris, et de ce faictez vostre farse; et au dreschier, chucquere largement.

To make Lenten Flans. Cook eels until dead, then remove the bones and all of the black part. Then grind it up in a mortar, [with] ginger, grains of paradise and saffron, distempered with almond milk or a little starch or rice flour; make your mixture with this. When dishing it up, sprinkle it generously with sugar.

[12.1] ms.: *freur*, with the first *r* changed to an *l*.

❖ II. Text, Translation & Commentary ❖   41

This eel flan, made expressly to answer Lenten food restrictions, begins a brief series of three lean pasties. Its recipe is vaguely echoed in a passage that the Bibliothèque Nationale copy of the *Viandier* has appended to a somewhat garbled one for fish milt and roe whose rubric reads, "To Make Flans and Pies in Lent that will Taste of Cheese." However, though the saffron and the sugar garnish are also present in the *Viandier*, most of the detail of the *Vivendier*'s version is not.

The initial step in the preparation of this dish is noteworthy: the eels are to be killed by cooking. An early *Regimen sanitatis* presents the rationale for this procedure, which originated in a perception that an eel was an aquatic relative of a snake and therefore potentially poisonous.[12.2] The live eel is to be drowned in wine, whose humoral nature is warm and dry and which will begin the necessary process of warming and drying this dangerous creature as soon as possible. The bourgeois *Menagier de Paris* makes use of an immersion in salt to accomplish the same end (Recipe 180), and further leaves the eel in the salt for three full days.

Wheaten starch is a standard ingredient in late-medieval cookery and seems to have been kept on hand in large kitchens. Typical directions for the domestic preparation of starch are found already in the late-thirteenth-century Anglo-Norman recipe collection called *Viande e claree*:

> Amydon. Pur fere amidon pur tut l'an, a tenyr taunt de tens come vos volez: pernez forment net, entur la seint Johan, e si le metez en un vessel e metez de bel ewe assez ove le forment neef jurs; e chescun jur serra le furment bien bien lavé e le ewe changé; e pus braez le bien, e pus metez le ariere en bel ewe e lessez le ester une nuyt, e pus colez hors le ewe; e pus metez le sus une lincele ver le solail dekes a taunt ke il seit sec; e pus, kaunt il est sec, pernez le e le metez en un net vessele. Si le tenez taunt come vos volez; e coverez le bien, e trenchez le en peces, &cetera.[12.3]

[12.2] ... *Par quoy est a doubter qu'il ne soient venimeux*. Patricia Willett Cummins, *A Critical Edition of Le régime tresutile et tresproufitable pour conserver et garder la santé du corps humain*, Chapel Hill (University of North Carolina), 1976, pp. 76–77. *Pour oster leur viscosité est bon de les bouter en vin toutes vives et illec les laissier mourir, et puis les preparer avecques saulse et galentin, qui est une espisse fort bonne.* (A galentine is seen below at Recipe 44.) Then, at the end of his directions for rendering eels suitably safe for eating, the author states, *Ainsi les preparent les cuysiniers des grans seigneurs*.

[12.3] Constance B. Hieatt and Robin F. Jones, "Two Anglo-Norman Culinary Collections Edited from British Library Manuscripts Additional 32085 and Royal 12.C.xii," *Speculum*, 61 (1986), p. 865; Recipe 21. For the period of our text, see an English recipe detailing a very similar operation in Constance B. Hieatt, "The Middle English Culinary Recipes in MS Harley 5401," *Medium Ævum* 65 (1996), p. 59; Recipe 23, *To make amydon*.

❖ ❖ ❖ ❖ ❖ ❖ ❖ ❖

[13. Pastez noyrois]

Pour faire pastez noyrois: prenez menuyse de luchs u d'aultre bon poisson, cuit[13.1], taillié par lopins, canelle et gingembre[13.2] deffait de vin aigre; et faictez petis patez; aucun les refrisent en huille.

To make Norse Pasties. Get pike minnows or those of some other good fish, cooked, cut into chunks, [mixed with] cinnamon and ginger tempered with vinegar; make little pasties. Some people sautee these in oil.

A second variety of lean pasty is the Norse Pie. This prepared dish appears to be of relatively venerable history, a recipe for it having appeared in the earliest known French collection, the *Enseignements* (part of Recipe 55; ll. 170–173: *Por fere pastez norreis*) and, remarkably, in very much the same version as is written in the *Vivendier* (see Appendix A, below). For a reason having undoubtedly to do with the provenance of the *Vivendier* recipes, this dish is copied only toward the end of the *Menagier de Paris* (Recipe 258: *Pastez norroiz*), and only among fifteenth-century compilations, the fifteenth-century additions in the Vatican manuscript of the *Viandier* (Recipe 208: *Pastez nourroys*) and the *Du fait de cuisine*, which dates from 1420 (Recipe 50: *Pastez nurriz*). Ingredients vary, perhaps depending upon whether the pies were to be served on meat or lean days: in the *Menagier*, the principal ingredient is chopped cod liver; Chiquart uses pork and chicken liver.

❖ ❖ ❖ ❖ ❖ ❖ ❖ ❖

[14. Aultre maniere de pastez et de flans]

[f. 156r (cxlii)] Pour faire aultre maniere de pastez et de flans: prenez tenche, carpres et d'aultre bon poisson, l'esventrés, sy le broyez tres-bien en un mortier avoec mie de pain et un poy de saffren pour donner couleur; destemprez tout de lait d'amandes; chucquere largement et au dreschier.

[13.1] The word *cuit* is in the masculine, seemingly agreeing with *poisson*. The rubricator's rough punctuation, which is normally fairly faithful to the sense of a passage, is present only after this word *cuit* and not before. The author may mean to offer an alternative between *menuyse de luchs* and *aultre bon poisson cuit*. In this case the *d'* of *d'aultre* is superfluous.

[13.2] ms: *gingebre*.

❖ II. Text, Translation & Commentary ❖ 43

To make another sort of Pasty and Flan. Get tench, carp and other good fish, eviscerate it, and grind it up thoroughly in a mortar with bread crumbs and a little saffron for colour; distemper it all with almond milk; sugar generously, and also on dishing up.

This is what we might term "your basic fish pie". The recipe is far from complex, and the dish makes no pretence to elegance. The generous dose of sugar, apparently both as an ingredient and as a serving garnish, tends to relate this pie or flan to the fifteenth century.

A comparison between this text and that of a recipe for *Pastez qui aient savor de formage* in the *Enseignements* (part of Recipe 55; ll. 174–178: see Appendix B, below) suggests the possibility that our scribe may have misread his source material — or that an error had crept into the manuscript tradition of this recipe before our scribe copied it. If the two texts do, in fact, represent the same recipe, then the phrase here, *prenez tenche, carpres* ... , corresponds to the phrase *prenez les leitenches de carpes* ... that is found in the *Enseignments*: this Recipe 14 may originally have been a means to offer the taste of cheese during Lent when, back at the beginning of the fourteenth century, cheese was a forbidden food. In this regard it may be noted that Recipe 12 is expressly (also) a dish suitable for Lent.

No similar dish is extant in the *Viandier*, although we know that without any doubt such a relatively plain fish pie must have been at least fairly common on medieval dining boards at this time. Its very simplicity may have obviated the need for a written recipe. The *Du fait de cuisine* of Chiquart offers a recipe for a somewhat more complex *Tartres de poyssons*: combining fish paste with fruit, nuts, spices and sugar, this dish reflected the slightly higher gastronomic level at which the chief cook to the Duke of Savoy normally operated.

❖ ❖ ❖ ❖ ❖ ❖ ❖ ❖

[15. Pour cuire un poisson en trois manieres]

Pour cuire un poisson en trois manieres et couleurs, c'est assavoir boulli, rosti et frit: envolepez la keuwe jusques au tierch d'un drap linge baignié d'esve salee, et en rostissant, et faictez feu egalment dessoubz le moillon; puis ayez bure fres ou huille bien chault, et quant vostre poisson sera bien rosti et cuit — mes gardez bien qu'il n'atouche point de feu dessoubz le tiers de la teste: mettez une tuille ou une piece[15.1] dessoubz; puis prenez vostre poisson tout droit et vostre huille ou bure chault en un pot et le frisiez tresbien jusques au

---

[15.1] A word or words appears to be missing here.

tiers ; et le coulouré d'or, d'argent et d'asur, la guelle ouverte jettant feu ; et servez comme un entremés, le boully a la saulce verd, le rosty a l'orenge espressee, et le frit a la cameline.

To cook a Fish in Three Ways and Styles[15.2], *that is, boiled, roasted and fried. Wrap the tail up to one-third of length of the fish with a piece of linen soaked in salted water, and cook it by roasting, bringing the fire to bear evenly beneath the middle [third]. Then get very hot fresh butter or oil and, when your fish is well roasted and cooked — but be careful that the fire doesn't touch the third at the fish's head: put a tile or a piece [of cloth] over it — then take your fish straight away along with your hot oil or butter in a pot and fry it well up to that third. And colour it with gold or silver or blue, with its mouth open and breathing fire. Serve it as an entremets, the boiled part with Green Sauce, the roasted with orange juice and the fried with Cameline.*

This three-way fish is identified as appropriately constituting an *entremets*. Certainly its relative complexity sets it off from the plainer, more fundamental fare with which this recipe collection has begun. A single fish, chosen in part for its exceptional length, is to afford the master and his guests the pleasure of being able to choose from among three different modes of preparation. As a supplementary source of delight, a sensation, the fish will breathe fire! This three-in-one "dish" occupies the realm of the marvellous.

The professional secrets involved in accomplishing this wonder are presented in some detail, albeit incompletely; the recipe is one of the longest copied in this book. Cooking the fish is merely the initial phase of the preparation of the *entremets*. In this operation the most interesting step is that in which the one-third at the tail is cooked by boiling: this is accomplished by means of heating a wet cloth in which that part of the fish is wrapped. The middle, exposed third of the fish is roasted at the same time and by the same fire.

What remains unexplained — the author apparently assuming that his reader, as a member of the profession, was conversant with the procedures, or else simply did not care about the technical questions, being able to leave them to inferior mechanics — is how a fish being served to a fifteenth-century table could be made to breathe fire. Fortunately, the phenomenon is far from uncommon at this time. Though the three-way fish in particular is not picked up by the *Viandier*, the fire-breathing trick is. In Recipe 219, among the fifteenth-century Vatican manuscript additions, a lion spouts flames by means of cotton and camphor in a bronze mouth. Chiquart likewise

---

[15.2] The word *couleurs* refers to the treatments to which the fish is subjected. Semantically the author's use of the word can be appreciated by considering the phrase "colours of rhetoric".

❖ **II. Text, Translation & Commentary** ❖   45

employs the technique, describing it in a little more detail (Recipe 10): the cotton is a wick for alcohol, "fire-water," this latter having been produced by multiple distillations of wine. For the *entremets* in which he thus lights up his master's banquet, Chiquart makes four creatures breathe fire: a boar's head, a swan, a piglet and, most interestingly, that very three-way fish (in Chiquart this is a pike) whose recipe we have here.

The saucing that Chiquart specifies is, for the boiled third of the pike, Green Sauce (as here, though expressly slightly tart with vinegar); for the roasted third, Green Sorrel Verjuice; and for the fried third, oranges (perhaps orange juice, as here for the roasted portion).

❖   ❖   ❖   ❖   ❖   ❖   ❖   ❖

[16. Souppe de cambrelencq]

[f. 156v] Pour faire une souppe de cambrelencq : prenez pain blancq et le mettez rostir sur le charbon par lesches, puis les mettez temprer en vin ; puis prenez chucquere ou grosse dragié, et le laissiez confir dessus ; aprés ayé vin boullant avoecq gingembre et canelle, jettez pardessus chauldement.

To make Chamberlain Sops. Get white bread and toast slices of it on the coal(s); then set them to temper in wine. Then get sugar, or coarse dragées, and let it macerate on top. After that, get boiling wine with ginger and cinnamon [in it], and pour it hot over top.

These Chamberlain Sops are known by that name in English recipe collections, for instance in the fifteenth-century manuscripts edited by Austin: *Soppes pour Chamberleyne* and *Soupes Jamberlayne*.[16] The recipe there is quite similar to that of the *Vivendier*, although the toast in the English version is covered with a spice powder (*blanche pouder*) rather than with the sugar or candied spices that we have here. The dish appears to have some relation to the *Bouruet* of Recipe 62, below.

The term *confir* in the text properly denotes the action of a sweet substance upon a foodstuff that is steeped in it, "to confect" or "to candy". Godefroy (9, 152a) glosses the verb *confire* (with a final *e*) as *préparer des fruits en les faisant séjourner dans une liqueur qui les pénètre et les conserve*. In this dish the sugar (or coarse

---

[16] Thomas Austin, *Two Fifteenth-Century Cookery-Books*, Early English Text Society, Original Series, 91, London (Oxford University Press), 1888 (repr. 1964), pp. 90 and 11 respectively. At p. 145 the editor of this English compilation also refers to the existence of a recipe called *Soupes Chamberlayn* in the MS Oxford, Bodleian, Douce 55 at N° 55, though without publishing this recipe.

spiced candy) is left to dissolve into the top of the wine-soaked slices of toast. The candied toast is then bathed, somewhat like a sop, in hot spiced wine.

❖ ❖ ❖ ❖ ❖ ❖ ❖ ❖

[17. Amplummus]

Pour faire un amplummus : prenez pommes pelleez et copez par morceaulx, puis mis boullir en belle esve fresce ; et quant il sont bien cuis, purez l'esve hors nettement, puis les suffrisiez en beau bure fres ; ayez cresme douce et moyeulx d'oels bien batus, saffren et sel egalment ; et au dreschier canelle et chucquere largement pardessus.

To make an Apple Sauce. Get peeled apples, cut into pieces, then set to boil in pure fresh water. When they are thoroughly cooked, drain off all of the water and sautee them in good fresh butter; get fresh cream and well beaten egg yolks and saffron, and salt judiciously. On dishing it up, cinnamon and sugar generously over top.

This is a variety of apple custard. It is not in the *Viandier*, but does have counterparts in English and German cookery, and in Chiquart's *Du fait de cuisine*. In this latter, the *Emplumeus de pomes* (Recipe 73) presents several variants: after boiling, the apples are not fried; instead of the cream and egg yolks, Chiquart uses almond milk; and there are no spices in the Savoyard version, although sugar is applied just as generously. An explanation of the generally simpler nature of Chiquart's applesauce may lie in the fact that, explicitly, he intends it to serve as a sickdish.

The recipe as it is copied in the *Vivendier* is not specifically "for the sick", yet this and the two dishes that follow are universally recognized as appropriate food for such a purpose. It would seem that this short sequence of three recipes could well have borne a rubric that would identify them as sickdishes.

Elsewhere we find similar recipes in the English *Applumoy* (*Forme of Cury*, Recipe 79; Hieatt and Butler, IV, Recipe 81), *Appulmos* and *Apulmose* (*Diversa servicia*, Hieatt and Butler, II, Recipes 17 and 35), *Apple Moys* and *Pomesmoille* (in Austin, pp. 30 and 113), *Apulmos* (*The Noble Boke of Cookry*, p. 121); the Anglo-Norman *Poumes ammolee* (Meyer, Recipe 9, and Hieatt and Jones, "B", Recipe 9); and in the German *Apfelmus* (*Guter Spise*, Recipe 69). The name *amplummus* probably derives from the German, being a combination of "apple" and "mush".

❖ ❖ ❖ ❖ ❖ ❖ ❖ ❖

[18. Comminee de poisson]

Pour faire une comminee de poisson : prenez du lait d'amandes et du pain blancq tempré dedens sans rostir, commin, gingembre et saffren ; passez tout parmy l'estamine, faictez boullir une onde ; qui ne soit trop cler ne trop espés ; et jettez par dessus vostre poisson, quel qu'il soit.

To make a Fish Cuminade. Get almond milk with untoasted bread tempered in it, cumin, ginger and saffron, all strained; bring it to a boil. It should be neither too watery nor too thick. Pour it over whatever fish you have.

The generic name of this preparation relates the dish to its principal ingredient, cumin. There were several varieties of cuminade in late-medieval cookery. The *Viandier* contains a Cuminade of Poultry (Recipe 12), a Cuminade of Almonds (Recipe 13), and a Cuminade of Fish (Recipe 75). This latter resembles the *Vivendier*'s version in its major respects (see Appendix B, below), although a clearly significant difference is that the *Viandier* points out its suitability as a sickdish.

In the fifteenth-century Vatican version alone of the *Viandier*, a reference to this recipe is appended after six others that are designated (in this and the Bibliothèque Nationale copy) as "For the Sick": *Pour malades*.

❖   ❖   ❖   ❖   ❖   ❖   ❖   ❖

[19. Coulich de malades]

Pour faire un coulich de malades : prenez le bran d'un poulet bien cuit, bien broyé et passé parmy l'estamine, deffait du boullon ; faictez boullir ; vin un poy, sel et chucquere.

To make an Invalid's Cullis. Get well cooked chicken brawn, ground, distempered with the broth and strained. Boil this, [with] a little wine, salt and sugar.

The generic name *coulis*, cullis, derives from the straining process to which the ingredients are subjected. Cotgrave defines a *potage coulis* or simple *coulis* as "a cullis, or broth of boiled meat strained; fit for a sicke, or weake bodie." It is of a smooth texture, bland, readily digestible and considered nourishing.

The cullis had long been recognized in late-medieval cookery as one of the most suitable preparations for the sick. This present recipe for an Invalid's Cullis is, indeed, the first of the series of six sickdishes in every copy of the *Viandier*; there it bears the title *Couleis d'un poulet*. In our collection it is the third and last of the more modest series of sickdishes. The inclusion of sugar in this dish is considered highly appropriate in a dish for the sick; at the same time it is an indication of the relatively late date of this recipe.

[20. Brouet de canelle]

[f. 157r (cxliii)] **Pour faire un brouet de canelle: cuisiez tel grain que vouldrez en vin et en esve, et despechiez par lopins et suffrisiez en beau sain; puis prenez amandes bien laveez sans peller, broyeez et passeez, destempreez de bon boullon, gingembre, clou et graine, deffait de vergus; faictez tout boullir ensamble, et vostre grain avoecquez, une onde seulement.**

To make a Cinnamon Broth. Cook whatever meat you like in wine and water, chop it up into chunks and sautee it in good rendered lard. Then get well washed, unpeeled almonds, ground and strained and distempered with good bouillon; get ginger, cloves and grains of paradise, distempered with verjuice. Bring everything just to a boil together along with your meat.

With this recipe the compiler of the *Vivendier* initiates a substantial series of so-called broths. A broth is normally a seasoned liquid in which a meat is cooked and which is poured over meat as it is served — as distinct from being served in bowls along with the meat, in order to function as a dipping sauce for it. For our author the recipe is a general-purpose one, as are a good number of the recipes in the opening pages of his collection. He presents it as suitable for any meat (*tel grain que vouldrez*).

For the author of the *Viandier*, however, the *Brouet de canelle* is a preparation expressly for poultry. All six of the broths at this point in the *Vivendier* have counterparts in the *Viandier*; even the sequence of broths in both works is the same, although in the *Viandier* several other broths and non-broths expand the series. A juxtaposition of the two versions of Recipe 20 (Appendix B, below) points up an anomaly in the *Vivendier*'s rendition of it: someone has omitted the cinnamon from among the ingredients of this Cinnamon Broth.

[21. Brouet rousset sur tel grain que vouldrez]

Pour faire brouet rousset sur tel grain que vouldrez: prenez ognons tailliez par roelles et persin effueillié — sy le suffrisiez en beau sain de lard; prenez pain harlé deffait de bon boullon et passé parmy l'estamine, gingembre, canelle, clou, graine, vin et vergus; faictez boullir

❖ II. Text, Translation & Commentary ❖ 49

tout ensamble, et vostre grain comme dessus ; et soit vostre[21.1] brouet roux.

To make a Russet Broth for over any meat you wish. Get sliced rounds of onions and parsley leaves, and sautee this in good rendered lard; get toast distempered in good bouillon and strained, ginger, cinnamon, cloves, grains of paradise and verjuice; boil everything together along with your meat, as above. It should be a real Russet Broth.

This *Brouet rousset* is modelled to some extent upon the procedures of the previous recipe. The meat (again, undifferentiated) is to be cooked with the fried onions (as in a *civé*[21.2]) and parsley. The thickener to be used in this sauce varies from version to version: the toast of the *Vivendier* is liver (presumably ground) in two of the *Viandier* copies, and bread and liver in the two others.

❖ ❖ ❖ ❖ ❖ ❖ ❖ ❖

[22. Brouet d'allemaigne de char ...]

Pour faire brouet d'allemaigne de char de connir, de poullaille ou autre : soit despechié par pieches et suffrit avoec ognons menu hachiez ; prenez lait d'amandes grant foison, gingembre, canelle, nois muscades, graine et saffren et faictez tout boullir ensamble avoeques bon boullon, et jettez par dessus vostre grain.

To make a German Meat Broth of rabbit, of chicken or of some other meat. It should be cut up into pieces and sauteed with finely chopped onions; get a lot of almond milk, and ginger, cinnamon, nutmeg, grains of paradise and saffron; boil everything together with good bouillon. Pour it over your meat.

This German Broth appears in both collections. In the *Viandier* the preparation is exclusively for rabbit or poultry, whereas our version more usefully allows any meat to form its basis.

This German Broth bears some resemblance to the *civé*, for which in the *Viandier* we find versions for veal, for hare and for rabbit (Recipes 28, 29 and 30). Both sautee the bits of meat with onions, use a range of spices and are of a

---

[21.1] ms.: *bie* with a superscript. There is evidence of some hesitation here: *bien* is normally abbreviated by our scribe as *bn* with a superscript; *vostre* is abbreviated as *vre* with a superscript. The text from which this recipe was copied likely read ... *et soit bien roux* at this point (see Appendix B); the word *bien* may have been abbreviated as *bie* with a nasal superscript. By inserting the word *brouet*, our scribe opted for the word *vostre*.

[21.2] See the *Viandier*'s *Civé de veel*, Recipe 28.

yellowish colour — this latter feature being expressly stipulated by the *Viandier*. A primary distinctive feature of the German Broth, however, is its greater blandness: it uses "a great deal" of almond milk (although with some verjuice in the *Viandier*), whereas the *civé* is highly spiced and uses vinegar.

It is quite likely that the name of this preparation originated in the primary role that almonds play in it. In a similar dish in the *Enseignements*, entitled *Blanc brouet de gelines* (Recipe 29; ll. 105–110)[22], the French word for "almonds" is written as *alemandes* — as it is consistently throughout that compilation. An oral confusion with the word for "German" is understandable, particularly if the *Vivendier*'s dish were at some time called simply *Brouet d'alemandes*.

❖ ❖ ❖ ❖ ❖ ❖ ❖ ❖

[23. Soultil brouet d'engleterre]

[f. 157v] **Pour faire un soultil brouet d'engleterre: prenez grosses chastaigne**[23.1] **cuittez, bien pelleez, moyeulx d'oes crus, foye de porc, broyé tout ensamble, destempré de boullon ou d'esve tieve, passé parmy l'estamine; prenez gingembre, canelle, clou, graine, espic, poivre long, garingal et saffren, et faictez tout boullir ensamble.**

To make a Subtle English Broth. Get large chestnuts, boiled and carefully peeled, raw egg yolks and pork liver; everything is ground together, distempered with bouillon or with warm water, and strained. Get ginger, cinnamon, cloves, grains of paradise, spikenard, long pepper, galingale and saffron, and boil everything together.

The qualification "subtle" refers to the consistency of this preparation. The components of this broth have been reduced to the finest particles, and as a consequence the dish is felt to be more readily digestible. The act of digestion must convert foodstuffs into various bodily humours, chyle and eventually blood; for this the digestive processes must be able to break all foods down and make as intimate a contact with their substance as possible. As in the cullis which is intended for serving to a sick person (Recipe 19, above), all of the ingredients in the Subtle English Broth are ground and strained through a fine sieve, thus assisting eventual digestion, although the broth, by its nature as an everyday dish for the healthy, is a somewhat thicker and more complex mixture than the cullis.

The essential ingredients here are chestnuts, egg yolks and pork liver. The last two of these ingredients make a thick mixture, particularly after it has boiled. The herb spikenard and the spices galingale and long pepper are not common in the

---

[22] This recipe turns up in the *Viandier* (Recipe 19) as *Blanc brouet de chappons*.
[23.1] ms.: *sic*.

standard cookery in French recipe collections; their use here may be evidence of an English origin of this broth.

The *Vivendier*'s text requires the egg yolks to be are raw; this seems a reasonable reading. An early copy of the *Viandier* seems to have misread the word *crus*, writing instead *cuis*[23.2], and made the yolks hard-boiled ever thereafter. Clearly this peculiarity of the yolks bothered several later copyists: one version tried to explain that the yolks are cooked "*in* a little pork liver"; another supplied wine in which to boil them in order to cook them.

Although no version of the recipe says so, we may suppose that this broth is to be served as a garnish on some sort of meat.

❖   ❖   ❖   ❖   ❖   ❖   ❖   ❖

[24. Brouet de vergus]

Pour faire brouet de vergus : cuisiez tel grain que vouldrez en esve, vin et vergus le plus ; et pain passé, tempré en vergus, et moyeulx d'oes, espicez — gingembre, graine et poivre long ; faictes boullir tout ensemble, bien assavouré de sel, et qu'il passe le vergus ; jettez par dessus vostre grain bien suffrit en beau sain de lard.

To make Verjuice Broth. Cook whatever meat you like in water, wine and, for the most part, verjuice. Get sieved bread tempered in verjuice, and egg yolks and spices — ginger, grains of paradise and long pepper; boil everything together, well seasoned with salt; the verjuice should predominate. Pour it over your meat, which has been well sauteed in fine rendered lard.

In Verjuice Broth, as its name and its recipe make clear, the flavour of verjuice must predominate. Yet the recipe also involves a mixture of spices; and two of the extant *Viandier* copies suggest that rendered lard should be the frying medium for the meat in order to impart even more flavour to the dish.

The meat in this preparation undergoes a double cooking: a boiling (with verjuice) and a sauteeing (in rendered lard). The spicy verjuice mixture is a serving sauce.

❖   ❖   ❖   ❖   ❖   ❖   ❖   ❖

[23.2] The copyist had just written *chastaignes cuites* several words before.

[25. Brouet vergay]

Pour faire brouet vergay : cuisiez tel grain que vouldrez en vin et en esve ou bon boullon de beuf, et du lard pour donner goust ; prenez pain passé deffait dudit boullon, persin, sauge et moyeulx d'oes, fin fromage qui voelt, et vergus, gingembre et saffren un poy pour faire vergay ; faictez tout boullir ensamble ; et jettez par dessus vostre grain — mais qu'il soit bien suffrit.

To make Gaudy-Green Broth. Cook whatever meat you like in wine and water or good beef bouillon, with some lard for flavour. Get sieved bread distempered with that bouillon, parsley, sage, egg yolks, fine cheese if you wish, verjuice, ginger and a little saffron to make it a bright green; boil everything together. Pour it over your meat after this has been well sauteed.

This broth is identified by its distinct colour. The term *vergay* — which we may properly render quite literally in English as "cheery green" — describes a bright green or a yellow-green that in late-medieval cookery was conventionally produced by combining colourants for green and yellow. Here, as usual, the green is obtained from the herb parsley; occasionally in some recipes sage may be combined with the parsley. For the yellow, a favorite culinary colour, cooks relied almost universally upon saffron, to which egg yolks could also be added by way of reinforcement.

As with the previous dish, the meat must first be boiled and then sauteed. The serving sauce is then poured over it.

❖ ❖ ❖ ❖ ❖ ❖ ❖ ❖

[26. Soupe crottee]

[f. 158r (cxliiii)] **Pour faire une soupe crottee : prenez belle esve en une payelle et le faictez boullir ; puis prenez fin fromage cras taillié par dez quarez et pain blanc pareillement, et du vin pour donner goust ; mettez dedens celle esve et faictez tout boullir ensamble.**

To make a Lumpy Sops. Get pure water in a pan and boil it. Then get fine fat cheese cut into cubes and white bread similarly cut, and wine for flavour; put these into the water and boil everything together.

The word *crotte* is glossed by Cotgrave as " ... The dung, excrements, or ordure of Sheepe, Goats, Conies, Hares, &c": in the modern vernacular we might say "crud". If this sense is that of dish's name, then it must be intended to evoke the appearance of the dish or an impression of its consistency. Figuratively, when the cubes of fat cheese boil in the water and wine, they might well end up looking a little like small, lumpy animal droppings. The analogy would not seem to do too much for a modern appetite, however.

It is tempting to relate the word *crottee* to the English genre *crustade* (ultimately, with a metathesis of the *r*, to become *custard*), but such dishes all clearly derive from the pastry crust which is basic to their nature. Alone the Italian *Crustata* of the Wellcome manuscript (Recipe 62) seems not to be a pie: it is a pudding, or custard, of thickened, sweetened almond milk incorporating spices and various fruits.

Generically the dish in our recipe is a sort of sop. Just how the cheese *crottes* were to be served is not explicit in the recipe; the author probably felt it sufficient merely to indicate the genre in the dish's name. What a contemporary reader would realize is that the contents of the boiling pot are to be served over a thick slice of bread or toast; this would be, properly, a sop. (The Neapolitan Collection has a *Crostata de caso e pane* at Recipe 94, not qualified as a "sop" but in which cheese is melted over slices of dry toast.) See other varieties of sop at Recipes 16, above, and 48 and 62, below.

❖ ❖ ❖ ❖ ❖ ❖ ❖ ❖

[27. Civet de carpres]

Pour faire un civet de carpres: mettez cuire les carpres en esve, sel largement et, quant elles sont cuittez, tirez les hors sur une belle nappe; prenez pain blancq harlé rousset, tempré en vin et ou plus gras du boullon, passé parmy l'estamine, espices communes, et saffren pour ly donner couleur; faictez tout boullir ensemble avoec des ognons fris en bure; mettez vos carpres en une[27.1] telle et jettez vostre brouet par dessus.

To make a Carp Civet. Set the carp to cook in water with a lot of salt; when they have cooked, take them out onto a clean cloth. Get lightly toasted white bread, tempered in wine and the fattest of the bouillon and sieved, common spices and saffron for colour; boil everything together, along with onions that have been fried in butter. Set your carp in an earthenware dish and pour your broth over top of them.

A *civet* or *civé* is generically a dish whose essence is onions, *cepæ* in Latin. They are sliced or chopped, then fried and mixed with some other main ingredient.

[27.1] ms: *vne*, with a superscript.

Here the sauce containing the fried onions is apparently to be "cast over" the drained carp. This sauce is applied not at the moment of serving the fish, which the recipe might suggest, but in order for the fish to undergo a final stage of preparation, boiling in a pot or earthenware dish (*une telle*). The civé is not a foodstuff and sauce, like a *brouet*, but a foodstuff *in* an onion-based mixture.

The *Viandier* does not have a carp or fish *civé*, but only civets for oysters (Recipes 82 and 148) and mussels (Recipe 150) and for meats and fowl. In any case the carp made its way into western Europe only in the course of the fourteenth century[27.2]; its presence in the *Vivendier* suggests a relatively late source for this recipe.

❖ ❖ ❖ ❖ ❖ ❖ ❖ ❖

[28. Poree en lait d'amandes]

Pour faire poree en lait d'amandes : prenez anguille[28] pourbouliez, et poree de bettez et de cresson, puis tirez vos anguilles et poree dehors ; ayez lait d'amandes et du plus gras de vostre boullon, faictes boullir en un pot, assavouré qu'il soit de bon sel ; mettez vostre poree dedens et anguilles boullir une onde, puis si les drechiez chaudement.

To make a Poree in Almond Milk. Get parboiled eels and greens of chard and cress, then take out your eels and greens. Get almond milk and the fattest of your bouillon, boil these in a pot flavoured with good salt; put in your greens and eels to boil briefly. Serve them hot.

This recipe is not in the *Viandier*. There is indeed a *Poree de cresson* at Recipe 153, but for this dish cress and beet greens are boiled, chopped, fried and re-boiled in almond milk; cheese and butter are optionally included outside of lean days. There is no mention of any meat or fish being involved here, whether in or under this *poree*.

❖ ❖ ❖ ❖ ❖ ❖ ❖ ❖

[29. Gellee de poisson]

[f. 158v] Gellee de poisson — carpres, tenches, brasmes, turbot et aultre bon poisson : soit bien affaittié et cuit en vin et en esve, puis le tirez hors du boullon sur une belle nape pour esgoutier quant il sera

---

[27.2] See Richard C. Hoffmann, "Environmental Change and the Culture of Common Carp in Medieval Europe," *Guelph Ichthyology Review*, 3 (May 1995), pp. 57–85.

[28] ms.: *sic*, without a plural *s*.

❖ II. Text, Translation & Commentary ❖

bien cuit; prenez espices — gingembre, canelle, clou, graine, saffren, espicq, garingal, deffaict[29.1] de puree de pois; mettez tout boullir ensamble; et se vous veez qu'il soit trop espés, sy le coulez devant le feu; puis dreschiez vostre grain em[29.2] plas bien clers et luisans, et jettez par dessus chaudement; puis assez vos plas en lieu froit sur le bel sablon; aucun y mettent des amandes pelleez et des petittez foellez de laurier doreez et argenteez, et en servent comme d'un entremés.

Pour faire .lx. escuelles de gellee y fault:[29.3]
.x. onches de grains[29.4] de paradis;
item, .vi. onches de macis;
item, .iii. onches de nois muscades;
item, .iiii. onches de gingembre;
item, une onche de clou;
item, .vi. onches de canelle;
item d'espic et garingal, .ii. onches de chascun.

Fish Jelly — carp, tench, bream, turbot and other good fish. It should be well dressed and cooked in wine and water; then take it out of the bouillon onto a clean cloth to drain. When it is thoroughly cooked, get spices — ginger, cinnamon, cloves, grains of paradis, saffron, spikenard and galingale, distempered with pea puree; set everything to boil together. If you see that it is too thick, take it off the fire and strain it. Then set out your fish in bright shining platters and pour the broth hot over it; then put your platters in a cool place on clean sand. Some people garnish this dish with peeled almonds and little laurel leaves painted gold and silver, and serve it up as an entremets.

To make 60 bowls of jelly you need:
10 ounces of grains of paradise
likewise, 6 ounces of mace
3 ounces of nutmeg
4 ounces of ginger
one ounce of cloves
6 ounces of cinnamon
2 ounces each of spikenard and galingale.

[29.1] ms.: *deffaitt*.
[29.2] ms.: *sic*.
[29.3] Exceptionally, each item in this list of ingredients is given a separate line in the manuscript. With this spacing the recipe fills the page to its foot.
[29.4] ms.: *sic*.

Fish jelly is a common culinary preparation in the late Middle Ages. Few recipe collections omit a recipe for it, although, like most of the very common dishes of this time, the recipes for this and other jellies are apt to vary widely from collection to collection, this largely because of minor ingredients which optionally might enter into any particular elaboration of it. Its preparation was universally recognized as a delicate operation, demanding the full attention of the cook. Even the Arab physician originally responsible for the *Tacuinum sanitatis*[29.5] seems to have been aware that jelly was not easy to make: "The blood that [jelly] produces is in some ways coldish, but it is particularly good for the secretion of bile which is the special property of gelatin. For this reason cooks should prepare it with skill and care . . . ." The printed *Viandier* is a little more insistent upon the cook's attentiveness during this particular operation: *Qui fait gelee, il ne fault dormir.*[29.6]

The principle of this or any jelly is that an animal or fish is selected that is known, empirically, to have on its skin or in its bones a source of animal gelatin. This gelatin is extracted into a solution, usually by boiling; various other ingredients — condiments and meats — are added to this, and then the whole mixture is allowed to set, normally a recipe will direct "in a cool place."

Four fish are named as a suitable starting-point for this Fish Jelly, even though our author adds, " . . . or some other good fish." The *Viandier* defines a little more usefully just what is meant by this phrase "good fish": the fish suitable for making jelly is the one *qui porte limon*, that is, "whose skin has a mucilaginous coating." In fact we find a reference to *poissons de limon* in the poetic plague tractate, attributed to the physician Jaque des Pars, that is copied in the Kassel manuscript immediately after the *Vivendier*: this sort of fish appears among the foodstuffs that one ought to avoid during a time of plague.[29.7] The slimey coating that in Old French is designated as *limon* is rich in protein and is the element that will be responsible for the phenomenon of jelling. The poet Eustache Deschamps identifies carp and barbel as being *lymoneux* — that is, particularly rich in this external mucus.[29.8]

[29.5] Ibn Botlan, or Ellbochasim, died in Antioch some time after 1068. For the recipe for *geletina* in this health handbook see Judith Spencer, tr., *The Four Seasons of the House of Cerruti*, New York and Bicester (Facts On File Publications), 1984, p. 50.

[29.6] "The person who makes jelly mustn't drowse." *Gelee de poisson*, in the Pichon and Vicaire edition of the *Viandier de Guillaume Tirel dit Taillevent*, p. 189.

[29.7] See the text of this medical counsel in Appendix C, below.

[29.8] *Œuvres complètes de Eustache Deschamps*, ed. Marquis de Queux de Saint-Hilaire and Gaston Raynaud, 11 vols., Paris (Firmin Didot), 1878–1903; Vol. 8, p. 339.

Jelly was valued in late-medieval cookery primarily as a preservative. For that purpose the secondary ingredients that were dissolved with the gelatin had normally to possess dry and warm qualities; this was, indeed, the nature, in varying degrees of strength, of a good range of the spices, so that we find special attention being paid to the selection of spices that were to be included in any jelly. The spikenard and galingale, which appear in the *Vivendier*'s spice list and in that of the *Enseignements* (Recipe 53; ll. 154–160), are found in the *Viandier* only in the relatively late Vatican manuscript copy. On the other hand, long pepper, seen in the *Enseignements* and faithfully in every copy of the *Viandier*, is not included by the *Vivendier*'s compiler. The choice of spices in a jelly or galantine was likely influenced to a good extent by contemporary taste, and undoubtedly also by relative cost or availability.

Here in the *Vivendier* a separate paragraph is devoted to enumerating those spices and — most exceptionally in this collection and elsewhere — in stipulating the precise quantities of each that should be employed. The precision with which the quantities are indicated make this annex a significant feature that distinguishes this and the following recipe. It seems clear that the compiler is indebted to a relatively recent source for these two recipes, or perhaps to his own professional experience (or that of his cook). Concerning the quantities that are specified, we may observe that, although the total amount to be prepared of each dish is different — sixty bowls in the case of the Fish Jelly (of which some are likely to be set aside for future use) and twenty bowls of the Wheaten Gravy — the "dose" of spices is by no means extravagant. The modesty here of the author's use of spices belies the blanket charge that medieval cookery was over-spiced.

All copies of the *Viandier* indicate that this preparation is a *Gelee de poisson ... ou de char* — thus making the recipe do double duty. The recipe in the *Enseignements*, as in the *Vivendier*, is for only a *Gelee de pesson*. Our text is alone in calling for pea puree as a macerating liquid for the spices; the specification of pea puree is appropriate, it being a standard lean-day liquid for this purpose.

The over-all quantity of sixty bowls of Fish Jelly is an amount that far exceeds the quantities prepared by other recipes in this collection. On the one hand this relatively large amount suggests the likelihood that some portion of this jelly was intended for keeping in the larder over some length of time. On the other hand it invites us to guess that this, and the following recipe, despite manifestly belonging to the traditional *Viandier* canon, owe their immediate origin to a treatment and copy which are separate from that extant tradition.

❖   ❖   ❖   ❖   ❖   ❖   ❖   ❖   ❖

[30. Grenee fourmentee]

[f. 159r (cxlv)] **Pour faire une grenee fourmentee : mettez du ble cuire** a mort, puis coulez l'esve hors nettement et laissiez reffroidier ; puis ayez lait de vache[30.1] nouvellement trait et le mettez boullir en un noef pot ; et quant il est sur le point de fremir, jettez vostre fourment dedens petit a petis en remuant dilligamment ; et quant tout est ens, tirez le pot arriere du feu ; puis ayez moyeulx d'oes bien batus, et les gernons nettement hostez, saffren et fleur d'amidun[30.2], et tout ce passé parmy l'estamine ; faictez boullir tout ensamble tant qu'il soit si espés que le[30.3] louce se puist tenir droite ou moillon ; puis le tirez arriere du feu et jettez dedens bure et sel egalment ; et qu'il soit de belle couleur.

Pour faire .xx. escuelle de grenee formentee, fault un[30.4] quartron d'oes ;

item, de garingal, de macis, de cloux, de gingembre, de saffren, de nois muscades, de silion, de poivre et sourmetaine — de chascune une once ;

item, une livre de chucquere,[30.5]

une livre d'amigdum[30.6],

et demie livre de bure.

To make a Wheaten Gravy. Set some wheat to boil until it bursts [no more water is taken up], drain the water off from it and let it cool. Then get freshly drawn cow's milk and set it to boil in a new pot; when it is just about to bubble, throw your wheat into it little by little, stirring attentively. When it is all in, draw your pot back off the fire. Then get well beaten egg yolks with their treads cleanly removed, with saffron and good starch, all this strained; boil everything together until it is so thick that the spoon can stand up in the middle of it. Then pull it back off the fire. Add butter and salt judiciously. It should be of a fine colour.

To make 20 bowls of Wheaten Gravy you need:

　　　　twenty-five egg [yolks]

[30.1] ms.: *bache.*

[30.2] The final nasel is represented by a superscript. *Cf.* toward the end of this recipes where the word is spelled out *amydum*.

[30.3] Either the article here is *li* or, more likely, the letter *e* of *le* is incomplete, its upper stroke not having been clearly penned.

[30.4] The scribe has written the word *un*, with a clear letter *n*. The rubricator then added dots before and after, in order to indicate a numeral, and put strokes above the two bars of the *n*; he understood the number .vii. The word *quartron* has no *s*; if the text were to read .vii., the quantity of egg yolks intended would be 175.

[30.5] Beginning with this line, the last three lines of this recipe are short, as each ingredient is given a separate line, perhaps in order to fill to the foot of the page.

[30.6] ms.: *sic.*

> one ounce each of galingale, mace, cloves, ginger, saffron, nutmeg, chervil, pepper, laserwort
> one pound of sugar
> one pound of starch
> one-half pound of butter.

In early French cookery, the origin and sense of the words *grané*[30.7] and *gravé* are moot, although the first form is apparently related to the word *grain*, meaning the principal meat of a prepared dish. The first term is clearly the one which our scribe has written in the *Vivendier*, twice in this recipe, with an unmistakable *n* rather than a *v* in its middle. The same word with its *n* recurs in Recipe 53, below: *Potage grenné*. In this second instance, because of the double consonant there can be no doubt as to the scribe's intentions.[30.8] The feminine form of the generic name in the present recipe is interesting: it probably indicates that the dish is to be prepared after the fashion of a *un grané*.

The meaning of the qualification in this title would seem to identify the dish as one in which wheat constitutes the *grain*, or "substance", normally in it. Normally in a *grané* or *gravé* the meat is reduced to small chunks; the texture of the dish is therefore somewhat lumpy. Here, however, the wheat gruel and egg yolks seem to form quite a smooth consistency. (Later, in Recipe 53, the *potage grenné* likewise has no meat, but only egg yolks and cheese.) It should be noted that no copy of the *Viandier* calls this dish a *grané* or *gravé*: there the recipe is named simply *Fromentee*.

What, then is the sense of the genre *grenée* by the time in the second half of the fifteenth century that the *Vivendier* was copied? Two suggestions can be made. One possibility is that it is simply a lean dish, continuing (and preceding) a series of preparations suitable for lean days; there is no meat in this particular variety of *grané*, which is merely a thick yellow porridge. A second possibility is that this particular composition of *fourmentee* is meant to be *suitable for use with* meat. A common gastronomic combination found in other recipe collections and menus is furmenty and venison and, its lean version, furmenty and porpoise. The *Viandier* recipe (Recipe 63) that is a counterpart to our Recipe 30 shows a final phrase, with optional ingredients for this furmenty, that may be significant: " ... And some people add in spices and saffron *and the bouillon from the venison*" (my italics: ... *et de*

[30.7] The word is also written *grainé*, *grainné*, *graigné* and *grené*.

[30.8] Of the occurrences of the two words in the *Viandier* manuscripts, all versions but that in the Mazarine copy prefer *gravé*, whereas the Mazarine scribe consistently writes *grané* or a variant of it. Again we may observe a certain *rapprochement* between the *Vivendier* and the *Mazarine* tradition of the *Viandier*.

l'eaue de la venoison). Without stating in the recipe that the furmenty is to be eaten with venison, the *Viandier* clearly assumes that it will be. For the *Viandier* it is a furmenty *for* meat, specifically, venison. That same sense may be indicated in our collection by the title *Grenee fourmentee*: this is a wheaten gruel for serving with meat.

Apart from its name, this recipe presents several other peculiar features. The specification of cow's milk is unusual; the recommendation to the cook that he ensure its freshness points up one of the dangers of relying upon any sort of animal milk. This precaution is not repeated in the *Viandier*. In our text alone, also, the spice list is explicit; in the various versions of the *Viandier* the mention of spices is limited to a mere summary: *espices* or *fines espices*. This reduction of an explicit and extensive list of ingredients, even though in the *Viandier* they are said to be optional, suggests that all four copies of the most famous work post-date the *Vivendier*. Furthermore, the author of the *Vivendier* insists, quite exceptionally, on the need to specify precise quantities for each of these spices.

Our version of the *Fromentee* is moreover unique by being creamy and very much thickened. Among its ingredients it includes butter, a favoured ingredient of our compiler; it also includes wheat starch — one pound of it for the twenty bowlsful of porridge, which seems like a generous amount. The mention of this starch is followed by an explicit, and graphic, insistence upon the thickness of the finished dish: the stirring spoon must be able to stand upright in the middle of it.

❖ ❖ ❖ ❖ ❖ ❖ ❖ ❖

[f.159v] **Chapittre de poissons** / *Chapter on Fish*

[31. Plays]

Plays doivent estre apparilliés par devers le dos au dessoubz de l'oreille, et bien laveez; cuitte comme un rouget; a sausse de vin et de sel; ou, qui en voet en potage, soit fritte.

Plaice should be cleaned towards its back beneath its gill[31], and washed well. It is cooked like a red mullet. It is eaten with a sauce of wine and salt. Should anyone like it stewed, it should [first] be fried.

With this recipe, and the rubric that precedes it, the collection moves into a new and clearly delineated section, a Chapter on Fish. Five fish alone constitute the subject matter of this chapter. All but the last one are, remarkably,

---

[31] That is, the knife should enter the belly of the fish at a point under its gill and work upward to the backbone and along it.

sea-fish. The habitat of the fish of the last recipe, the sturgeon, is both the sea and fresh-water rivers and lakes; the *Viandier* deals with sturgeon toward the end of its "flat sea-fish". The compiler of this set of recipes seems to have had access more to sea-fish than to fresh-water fish.

For organizational purposes in its extensive fish section, the *Viandier* recognizes three categories of fish and, apart from the copy in the Valais manuscript, inserts a rubric for each: fresh-water fish, round-bodied sea-fish and flat-bodied sea-fish. Here in the *Vivendier* only the last section is represented, and in the sequence (though with "omissions") in which these five fish appear in the larger collection. It is true that a sturgeon seems hardly classifiable as a "flat sea-fish", but in the *Viandier* this recipe precedes a catch-all, perhaps a fourth marine section, consisting of molluscs and crustaceans. The presence there of sturgeon may be the result simply of an oversight; or else that position may relate in some way to its occurrence here at the end of the *Vivendier*'s list of four flat sea-fish.

Plaice is a fish of the North Atlantic and western Mediterranean. Very common along North Sea shores, it is a shallow-water fish, living only down to 100 m. or so. In our collection the author uses its treatment as a model for the preparation of the three subsequent flat-fish that he will deal with. The nature of that treatment for plaice is to be noted, however. Our author (or scribe) writes (or copies) quite casually that the plaice is to be cooked "like a red mullet", this being a *round* sea-fish that has not been mentioned in this collection, and will not appear even later. Any reader of this recipe who happens not to be familiar with the standard treatment of red mullet, or who does not have access to a master chef or a text where advice could be sought, might be at a loss to prepare plaice.

Where does this textual mention of the *rouget* come from? Quite possibly the reference may be to "general knowledge": handling a red mullet might be "one of those procedures that every professional cook knows." Clearly, too, the reference may be that which made sense in some earlier copy of a sequence of fish recipes in which a recipe for red mullet existed and served as a model for, *inter alia*, a treatment of plaice. Unfortunately, our scribe just happened to skip this crucial earlier recipe for red mullet. In the *Viandier* the red mullet does in fact appear before the plaice, and the manner of its cooking does in fact explicitly serve as a model for a number of subsequent fish, including plaice. In the *Viandier*'s Recipe 120, for Gurnard, Red Mullet and Red Gurnard (*Gournault, rouget, grimondin*), we read: "Clean it out through its belly and wash it thoroughly; put it in the pan with salt on it, and water afterwards; cook it; eat it with Cameline Sauce." The significant element here, for our purposes, is that the fish, the red mullet, and likewise our plaice and later sole, ray and turbot (Recipes 32, 33 and 34), once slit, cleaned and perhaps cut up, are to be dredged in salt, seared in a pan and then boiled.

[32. Solles]

Solles doient estre apparilliez et cuitte comme plays, et mengié a la saulce vert ; et, qui voelt, soit rostie sans eschauder, ou fritte en huille sans enfariner.

Sole should be cleaned and cooked like plaice. It is eaten with Green Sauce. Should anyone wish, it may be roasted without having been scalded, or fried in oil without having being dredged in flour.

These directions for the preparation of sole abbreviate its details by referring back to the previous recipe, for plaice.

[33. Rayes]

Rayes soient apparilliez par le nombril, et gardez bien le foye ; sy despechiez la raye par pieches et cuisiez comme la plais, puis la pellez ; et mengiez aux aux camelins.

Ray should be cleaned through its belly hole — and be sure to keep the liver. Cut up the ray into pieces and cook it like the plaice; then skin it. Eat it with Cameline Garlic Sauce.

For its cooking the ray (like the previous and following fish) is to follow the procedure specified for the plaice (Recipe 31). The chunks of its flesh are to be coated with salt (perhaps dredged in it) and then seared and boiled. Only then, just before serving, is the skin to be peeled from the pieces.

No mention is made here of what is to be done with the ray's liver, so carefully removed before the fish is cooked. However, the *Viandier* makes clear from its earliest versions that the liver is to be cooked as well, although less than the ray itself. This special handling of the liver reveals an awareness of its special gastronomic value, a value which is exploited and enhanced in an appended passage in the Vatican version of this recipe for rayfish (Recipe 136; see Appendix A, below).

[34. Turbot]

Le turbot soit cuit et apparillié comme une[34.1] plais, et puis pellez par devers le dos ; a la sauce vert.

[34.1] ms.: *sic.*

Turbot should be cooked and cleaned like a plaice, and then skinned up towards its back. It is eaten with Green Sauce.

While the turbot continues (with the sole, Recipe 32) to refer the reader back to the first fish of this Chapter, the plaice (Recipe 31), the treatment is not altogether identical in this case. Expressly we are told here that the turbot is to be skinned *after* being cooked, rather than before. There has been no explicit mention of a skinning previously, only of the "cleaning" and washing that precedes the cooking of the fish.[34.2] In every case, for plaice, sole, ray and turbot, we may assume that the skin remains on the fish until it has been salted, seared in the pan and boiled.

❖   ❖   ❖   ❖   ❖   ❖   ❖   ❖

[35. Esturgon]

Esturgon: eschaudez, et fendez par le ventre et le teste fendez et copez en deux et tous les aultres tronchons que se puellent fendre fendus, et cuis en vin et en esve — que le vin passe ; quant il est cuit, mettez reffroidir ; et soit mengié au persin effueillié et au vin aigre par dessus.

Scald sturgeon and slit it open along its belly; split its head and cut it in two, and all the other chunks that can be are cleaved off. It is cooked in wine and water, with the wine predominating. When it is cooked, set it to cool. It should be eaten with parsley leaves and vinegar over top.

This last fish of the Chapter was highly respected by medieval gastronomes. In the *Enseignements* it occupies a unique position by having been copied as the leading item in the section of *Poissons de mer e d'eve douche* — but where, curiously, the following paragraphs deal with a wide range of lean prepared dishes.[35] The recipe for sturgeon in that collection begins, *Esturjon est un pesson real e*

[34.2] It may be noted, though, that the oldest extant copy of the *Viandier*, that which is found in the manuscript roll at the Archives of the Valais in Sion and which dates from the beginning of the fourteenth century, does not have the word *puis*. This text directs merely that the turbot is to be *appareilliez comme plais pelé vers le dos a la saulce vert*.

[35] This is Recipe 48 in Carole Lambert's edition, at ll. 125–128 in the Lozinski edition. It is obvious that the person transcribing these recipes in the *Enseignements* left a bit of a jumble in their logical sequence. At the end of his copy, just before his closing *explicit*, he tries to redeem himself by advising his reader: *Metez esturjon e ceu qui ensuet aprés congre: c'est droiz.* The Latin version of this collection, *Doctrine preparationis ciborum* (also edited by Carole Lambert in the same place), offers a much more reasonable sequence of recipes at this part of the work. See her Note 1 on p. 100.

doiet estre depechiez par pieches ... ; the remainder of the text shows only remote similarity to what we read in the *Vivendier*. Both the *Viandier* and the *Menagier de Paris* classify the sturgeon as a sea-fish.

The culinary treatment of the sturgeon has features that distinguish it from what has been written for the four previous varieties of fish. In particular we may note that this fish is to be reduced to chunks and that the flavour of wine is to be imparted to it as it cooks.

❖ ❖ ❖ ❖ ❖ ❖ ❖ ❖

[f. 160r (cxlvi)] **Chapittre de saulces** / *Chapter on Sauces*

[36. Saulce non boullie dicte cameline]

Saulce non boullie ditte cameline: canelle, gingembre, clou et graine et pain passé harlé bien noir, deffait de vergus, vin et vinaigre.

Unboiled sauce called Cameline. Cinnamon, ginger, cloves, grains of paradise, darkly toasted bread, sieved, distempered with verjuice, wine and vinegar.

The second general rubric of this recipe collection is found at this point: *Chapittre de saulces*. This heading is intended to comprise the following six recipes. Imbedded into two of the recipes themselves are two further local rubrics: the beginning of the present recipe announces a category which will be illustrated by this and the following two recipes: "Unboiled Sauces." At Recipe 39, its counterpart, "Boiled Sauces" will likewise group another three sauces. The division, therefore, between the two major categories of hot and cold sauces is deliberately and carefully maintained in this collection as in the *Viandier*, even though the representative recipes in each category are typically close to a modestly minimum number.

Cameline is a cold cinnamon sauce, of a medium brown colour, in which any other ingredients tend more or less to be optional and of less gustatory significance. It is the most commonly used of all late-medieval sauces, a staple in virtually any European cuisine. The next recipe suggests that a particularity of Cameline Sauce must have been a noticeable dose of vinegar.

❖ ❖ ❖ ❖ ❖ ❖ ❖ ❖

[37. Saulce aux aux camelins]

Aux camelins se font pareillement, mais il y fault dex[37] aux poingnant le vinaigre.

---

[37] ms.: *sic*. The word is intended to be either the numeral *deus*, or, perhaps more likely, *des*, the spelling of which has been influenced by the following word.

Cameline Garlic Sauce is similarly made, but it needs garlic buds cutting through the vinegar.

Following the basic Cameline Sauce, the compiler offers a variation on the same genre: Cameline Garlic Sauce. For this variety of Cameline the cook adds enough garlic to be noticeable above the vinegar.

❖ ❖ ❖ ❖ ❖ ❖ ❖ ❖

[38. Saulce aux aux blans]

Aux Blans: bien broyez, et mie de pain blancq, destemprez de vergus.

White Garlic Sauce. [Garlic is] well ground up, along with crustless white bread, distempered with verjuice.

As is often the case in the names of late-medieval culinary preparations, their colour helps to determine their name. Here, distinct from the brownish Camelines, the White Garlic Sauce is made of white bread and (presumably) a white verjuice.

❖ ❖ ❖ ❖ ❖ ❖ ❖ ❖

[39. Saulces boulliez — d'un poivre jaunet]

Saulces boulliez — d'un poivre jaunet: prenez pain harlé destempré de vinaigre et de vin, et le passez parmy l'estamine; espices — saffren, clou, poivre long, gingembre et graine; faictez boullir tout ensamble.

Boiled sauces: A Yellow Pepper Sauce. Get toast distempered with vinegar and wine, and strain it, along with spices — saffron, cloves, long pepper, ginger and grains of paradise. Boil everything together.

Yellow Pepper Sauce begins the selection of three representatives of the category "Boiled Sauces" in the *Vivendier* — just as this particular sauce opens a similar but longer chapter in the *Viandier*. The name of the sauce has nothing to do with the colour of the sort of pepper that is the principal ingredient here; rather, "yellow" (more properly, "yellowish") refers to the hue of the finished sauce, in which saffron is to be a colourant. It stands as distinct from the following variety of pepper sauce.

❖ ❖ ❖ ❖ ❖ ❖ ❖ ❖ ❖

[40. Saulce au poivre chault noir]

Poivre chault noir : pain brullé noir deffait de vin aigre et passé parmy l'estamine ; faictes boullir avoec poivre noir.

Hot Black Pepper Sauce. Burnt toast distempered with vinegar and strained. Boil this with black pepper.

As in the previous recipe, the colour refers less to the colour of the pepper — although black pepper is, indeed, to be used here — than to the darkness of the final sauce. For this black sauce the cook relies not only upon the black pepper but also upon dark ("burnt") toast.

❖ ❖ ❖ ❖ ❖ ❖ ❖ ❖

[41. Jansce de lait de vache]

Jansce de lait de vache : pain blanc tempré en[41.1] **lait, et mioefz d'oes passé parmy l'estamine, et gingembre blancq deffait de vergus; faictez tout boullir ensamble.**

Jance of Cow's Milk. White bread tempered in milk, strained egg yolks, and white ginger distempered with verjuice. Boil everything together.

The third and final hot ("boiled") sauce is a variety of Jance Sauce called Cow's Milk Jance. The Jances constituted the second major family of sauces in medieval Europe, after the Camelines. The Camelines were a cold, cinnamon sauce; the Jances were a hot, ginger sauce. It is perhaps surprising that this variation should be the sole representative of the whole of the family of Jance sauces — given, moreover the normally limited usefulness of animal milk in French cookery generally at this time. The presence once again of a dairy product as a primary ingredient strengthens a hypothesis that the origin of this collection lies in the north or northeast of France. This despite the curious omission of an explicit listing of cow's milk in our scribe's rendition of this recipe.

While the *Viandier* offers a recipe for a plain Jance (ginger, almond milk and verjuice: Recipe 168, *Jance de gingembre*), our compiler either did not think a plain Jance useful, or he may have felt its recipe too simple to be included in his assortment of recipes.

Plain Jance is normally made with verjuice, as it is in the *Viandier* and the *Menagier*. However, in neither work does the cow's milk version of this sauce

---

[41.1] The word *en* is repeated in the text.

❖ II. Text, Translation & Commentary ❖ 67

call for verjuice.[41.2] For this recipe, combining ginger, raw egg yolks and cow's milk, the *Menagier* indeed inserts a significant caution: rather than using raw yolks, "for fear [this combination] may turn, the yolks should be cooked, then ground and strained." The mixture of ginger and yolks is strained with the cow's milk, then heated. Yet, on the other hand, in neither of the other works does the Cow's Milk Jance call for a thickener of bread as does our present recipe. If not the result of a scribal error, the presence of verjuice here in the *Vivendier*'s *Jansce de lait de vache* may represent a deliberate and remarkable experimentation.

❖ ❖ ❖ ❖ ❖ ❖ ❖ ❖

[42. Crevesches]

Crevesches: on les doit bien laver et cuire en un pot bien couvert sans esve, avoec du vin — ou du vin aigre et de l'esve ou du vergus — et du sel egalment; et laissiez bien boullir si qu'il se puist escumer de lui meismes, puis les purer et tenir que bien couvertes [f. 160v] chauldement; puis mengier au sel et au vin aigre ou persin effueillié par dessus.

Crayfish. They should be carefully washed and cooked in tightly covered pot without water but with wine — or else in vinegar and water, or with verjuice — and salt judiciously. Let it boil to the point where it can be skimmed by itself, then drain them and keep them well covered and hot. Eat them with salt and vinegar with parsley leaves on top.

The options appropriate for a cooking liquid or liquids for crayfish are rather awkwardly set forth. When the rubricator punctuated the text, he placed a slash after *esvue*, after *vin* and after *vergus*: according to him, therefore, we should read: " ... cook in a well-covered pot without water, with wine, or vinegar and water or verjuice, and likewise salt ... ." This does, indeed, seem to present a reasonable way to understand the text as it stands. A possibility remains, though, that the option provided in the *Viandier* had become garbled, and that the mention of cooking in an oven became merely "cooking dry"; alternatively the crayfish would be boiled in wine, or in vinegar-and-water, or in verjuice.

❖ ❖ ❖ ❖ ❖ ❖ ❖ ❖

[41.2] Recipe 166, *Jance au lait de vache* in the *Viandier*, and *Jance de lait de vache* in the Brereton and Ferrier edition of the *Menagier de Paris*, at p. 261.

[43. Lamproye]

Lamproye: on la doit faire saignier par la guele, et hoster la langhe; et y convient boucter une brochette de bois dedens pour mieulx saignier — et gardez bien le sang car c'est sa gresse — puis le faitte esbrocher[43.1] comme une anguille, et rostir en une broche bien delié; puis prenez gingembre, canelle, graine, mughettes et un poy de pain harlé, tempré en vin et passé, et faictez boullir ensamble une heure ou tant; mettez vostre lamproye boullir avoecquez toute entiere une onde seulement; et ne soit pas trop noire vostre saulce.

Lamprey. It should be bled through its mouth, and remove its tongue; you should shove in a wooden skewer to bleed it better — and keep its blood for that is its grease. Then mount it on a spit like an eel and roast it on a very slender spit. Then get ginger, cinnamon, grains of paradise, nutmegs and a little toast, tempered in wine and strained; boil this together an hour or so. Put your lamprey whole into this to boil only briefly. Your sauce should not be too dark.

This and the following recipe for *Lamproye a la garentine* are paired as well in the *Viandier*. The text of both recipes is quite close to what is read in the *Viandier*.

No explicit direction is offered concerning the eventual use of the lamprey's blood.[43.2] In the Valais manuscript alone of the *Viandier*, however, the advice is appended: *metez du sanc boullir avecques* — that is, the reserved blood is to be put into the sauce and with the lamprey itself.

❖ ❖ ❖ ❖ ❖ ❖ ❖ ❖

[44. Lamproye a la garentine]

Lamproye a la garentine: faictez sangnier vostre poisson comme dessus, et gardez le sang; puis le cuisiez en esve, vin et vin aigre, et, quant elle sera cuite, tirez le ariere du feu et laissiez reffroidir;

[43.1] ms.: *esbroher*, clearly a scribal lapsus.

[43.2] The *Menagier* (at Recipe 185) amplifies this procedure for bleeding the lamprey. *Il est assavoir que les aucuns seignent la lamproye avant ce que ilz les estauvent, et aucuns les estauvent avant ce qu'ilz les seignent ne eschaudent. Pour la seigner, premierement lavez tresbien vos mains, puis fendez luy la gueulle parmy le menton* — id est *joignnant du baulievre* — *et boutez vostre doit dedens et arrachiez la langue; et faictes la lamproye seigner en ung plat, et luy boutez une petite brochecte dedens la gueule pour la faire mieulx saigner; ... et gardez ce sang, car c'est la gresse.*

puis le mettez sur une belle nappe ; prenez pain brullé deffait de vostre boullon, passé parmy l'estamine, et du sang de vostre lamproye ; faictez boulir tout ensamble et gardez bien qu'il n'arge ; puis le versez en une telle, et le mouvez tant qu'il soit refroidié ; prenez espicez — gingembre, clou, graine, canelle, mughettez, poivre long — desmellez ensemble, et mettez vostre poisson dedens.

Lamprey in Galantine. Bleed your fish as above, and keep its blood; then cook it in water, wine and vinegar. When it is cooked, take it off the fire and let it cool; then put it on a clean cloth. Get burnt toast, distempered with your bouillon and strained, and some of your lamprey's blood; boil everything together, watching that it doesn't burn. Then pour it into an earthenware dish and stir it until it has cooled; get spices — ginger, cloves, grains of paradise, cinnamon, nutmegs and long pepper — mix them together and put your fish into them.

A galentine is a variety of dark spiced jelly that is prepared — here, specifically for lamprey. Other uses of galentine involved pike.[44.1] As a dish it had been known for close to two centuries. See in Appendix B the *Galentine a la lampree* of the *Enseignements* — whose text is remarkably close to the *Vivendier*'s copy. The dish seems to have been equally well known beyond France: in Savoy in 1420 Chiquart lists *Galatine de lamproyes* in a menu[44.2], but provides no recipes for it, likely considering it to be too common a preparation; the *Forme of Cury*[44.3] and other English collections contain *Laumpreys in galyntyne* of one sort or another.

The vessel into which the jelling liquid is poured in order to cool and set, with the lamprey in it, is referred to in the text as *une telle*. In the *Viandier* an option of different containers is offered: a mortar or *une jatte*, "a bowl". For this latter, in the earliest manuscript, that of the Valais archives, there is an interesting qualification: *une geste de fust*, "a wooden bowl". The Mazarine manuscript has merely a "vessel". The *telle* of the *Vivendier* is likely an elongated, deep, earthenware dish, somewhat more appropriate for the purpose of jelling a whole lamprey.

❖   ❖   ❖   ❖   ❖   ❖   ❖   ❖

[45. Haricocq de mouton]

[f. 161r (cxlvii)] **Pour faire un haricocq de mouton : mettez le par lopins tout cru suffrire en beau sain de lard avoec ognons hachiez**

[44.1] The *Viandier* itself includes a Pike Galentine at Recipe 97.

[44.2] *Du fait de cuisine*, ff. 111r and 114r.

[44.3] Ed. Hieatt and Butler, Part IV, Recipe 130.

menu, vin et vergus et bon boullon, persin, polioel, ysope ; faictez tout bien boulir ensamble.

To make an Haricoc of Mutton. Set it raw, in chunks, to sautee in good rendered lard, along with finely chopped onions, wine, verjuice and good bouillon; at the end, [add in] pennyroyal and hyssop. Boil everything well together.

The dish known as *haricoc* is made only with mutton. The meat is first sauteed with onions — which makes one think of a *civé* — and then boiled, with herbs being added in.

Beyond France the dish seems to be known only in Catalonia where it turns up as a *Arricoch* among the recipes of the Valencian copy of the *Libre de sent soví* [45.1] and as *Potatge de nerricoch* in Ruperto de Nola's *Libre del coch* [45.2].

Concerning the unusual potherb *polioel* or pennyroyal, see the comment to Recipe 10, above.

❖ ❖ ❖ ❖ ❖ ❖ ❖ ❖

[46. Cretonnee de pois nouveaux]

Cretonnee de pois nouveaux : soient cuis jusques au purer, puis suffris en beau sain de lard ; prenez lait de vache et le boulez une onde en un noef pot ; ayez pain[46.1] **blancq tempré oudit lait, gingembre et saffren, tout passé parmy l'estamine ; puis ayez moyeulx d'oes bien batus et les gernons hostez, jettez dedens sur le point de fremir et vos pois dedens en remuant dilligamment ; puis ayez vostre grain — poulez par pieches — suffrit en sain de lard, et boullis une onde avoecques ; puis dreschiez chaudement.**

Cretonnee of New Peas. They should be cooked to a mush, then sauteed in rendered lard. Get cow's milk and bring it to a boil in a new pot. Have white bread tempered in that milk, along with ginger and saffron, everything strained. Then get well beaten egg yolks, with their treads removed, put them in as it is coming to a boil, along with your peas, stirring attentively. Then have[46.2] *your meat — chicken pieces — sauteed in rendered lard and boiled briefly with the rest. Then dish it up hot.*

[45.1] Ed. Grewe, Appendix I, Recipe 59.

[45.2] Ed. Leimgruber, Recipe 80. See also the *Potatge de meritoch* of Recipe 63 in the same collection. See Liliane Plouvier, "Les métamorphoses du haricot de mouton," in *Ambiance culinaire*, (January 1988), pp. 60–61.

[46.1] ms.: following the word *pain*, the letters *pla*, crossed out.

[46.2] This seems to be a rare causitive use of the verb *avoir*, equivalent to writing *faites suffrire*. In Recipe 54 we shall in fact read *Faictez grain suffrit* . . . .

❖ II. Text, Translation & Commentary ❖ 71

    Despite initial appearances, this dish bears some resemblance to the previous one: the meat (in this case chicken, in Recipe 45, mutton) is firstly fried in rendered lard and then boiled briefly with the other ingredients. In this case the other ingredients are fried peas and milk, thickened with bread and egg yolks.

    The *cretonnee* is closely related to the *gratunee* of Chiquart.[46.3]

❖ ❖ ❖ ❖ ❖ ❖ ❖ ❖

[47. Cretonnee de fevez]

Cretonnee de fevez se fait pareillement.

Cretonnee of Beans is done the same way.

    This variant *cretonnee* is the last recipe which points distinctly to a connection with the *Viandier*. It is perhaps significant that the directions are abbreviated to merely "The same as before" — as they are in the *Viandier* tradition itself.

❖ ❖ ❖ ❖ ❖ ❖ ❖ ❖

[48. Soupe de quaresme]

Soupe de quaresme: prenez puree de pois[48.1], et commin et saffren en poure; mettez en demi[48.2] quarte de puree et un hanap de vin — et se c'est vergus, s'en mettez mains; du sel a point; faictez boullir; sy le jettez sur les souppes bien chaudement.

Lenten Sops. Get pea puree, powdered cumin and saffron; put two quarts of puree and a goblet of wine — and if you use verjuice, put in less; some salt, judiciously. Boil. Pour it very hot over the sops.

    These Lenten Sops mark a new direction, both generically and in inspiration, for this collection. From this point on, the material in the book appears unrelated in any direct way to that of the *Viandier* tradition. The source (or sources) is (are) clearly elsewhere and for the most part entirely independent of that tradition.

    Though the sops described in this present recipe belong to a different genre than the compiler has been concerned with immediately before, they do make use once again of a legume, peas.

[46.3] *Une gratunee de pollas* in the *Du fait de cuisine*, Recipe 62.

[48.1] ms.: the *s* of *pois* has an exaggerated upper loop followed by the rubricator's red punctuation mark.

[48.2] ms.: apparently *dej* with a superscript slur.

[49. Rys en galles c'on dit "contrefait"]

[f. 161v] **Rys en galles con dit "contrefait": prenez farine blanche, et pour chascune escuelle un oef fres, sel et chucquere; hachiez tout enssamble ossi menu comme sel, puis le mettez seschier devant le feu; et quant il sera secq, ayez bon boullon gras sur le point de fremir et jettez dedens en remuant dilligamment; et du fin fromage gratté au dreschier par dessus.**

Joke Rice that is called Counterfeit. Get white flour and, for each bowlful [you will be making of the dish], a fresh egg, salt and sugar. Chop everything up together as fine as salt, then set it to dry in front of the fire. When it is dry, have good fat bouillon just on the point of boiling and put it in, stirring attentively. When dishing it up, fine grated cheese on top.

Rys en galles may be translated more or less literally as "Rice-in-Jest" or "Playful Rice". It is the first of three recipes which are for farinaceous preparations, somewhat resembling varieties of *pasta asciutta*.

Our author seems to use the term counterfeit a little hesitantly, as if perhaps he were not familiar with it or did not expect his reader to be familiar with it. Despite this, a surprising number of dishes in late-medieval cookery are in fact designated as "counterfeit". The sense of this qualification is that the dish is somehow a phony, that it does not contain some particular ingredient that the diner would expect. Normally this surprise would be occasioned by the principal ingredient mentioned in the dish's name: rather than what is expected, some other ingredient or combination of ingredients cleverly imitates this foodstuff. In a sense, such a dish is for that reason a sham, a fake.[49] Normally the substitution of ingredients is not deliberately fraudulent in nature: on lean days the cook is merely accommodating particular lean-day prohibitions in as pleasant and palatable a way as possible. In most cases such counterfeiting is carried out in the spirit of a game.

This Joke Rice, or Pretend Rice, actually has no rice in it. It is made of a mixture of flour and eggs, reduced to bits the size and shape of a grain of rice, and dried. These bits are, eventually, cooked like rice in a very hot bouillon. The

---

[49] Italian cooks seem to have had a predilection for such phony fare. Their Lenten dishes include counterfeit butter, counterfeit ricotta cheese, and counterfeit eggs: see, for example, Martino, Recipes 154, 153 and 266, respectively. The *Menagier* has a recipe in which beef pretends to be bear (Recipe 147), and others in which fruit and nuts are used *pour contrefaire le pignolet* (Recipe 260), and veal masquerarades as pseudo salmon (Recipe 206).

bouillon is described as fat or greasy: the *contrefait* rice is consequently not a lean preparation.

❖   ❖   ❖   ❖   ❖   ❖   ❖   ❖

[50. Rys en gresse]

Rys en gresse : soit bien eslit et lavé, puis mis essuer devant le feu ; et quant il est bien secq, mettez le cuire en bon boullon gras de chapon ou aultre, et en quaresme en lait d'amandes ; bien chucqueré au dreschier.

Rice in Grease. Carefully culled and washed, then set to dry before the fire. When it is quite dry, set it to cook in good fat capon bouillon or in some other sort of fat stock; in Lent in almond milk. When dishing it up, it is sprinkled well with sugar.

Rice in Grease seems an inappropriate name for this dish, unless we accept that the "greasiness" of the preparation is in reality the only peculiarity of what is, all in all, a remarkably simple dish. The name seems all the less appropriate when for this same cooking the Lenten version of *Rys en gresse* makes use of a particularly lean and grease-free almond milk.

Curiously, the presence early in the *Buch von guter spise* of a *Ris von Kriechen* ("Greek Rice": Recipe 5), which is very similar to the dish of the present recipe, may both confirm the French title and indicate the relatively long existence of this dish. This German version was written about 1340. "This is called Greek Rice. Take rice and boil it in spring water. When it is half cooked, pour away the water and then cook the rice in pure lard. Then pour away the lard and cover the rice with sugar. Serve it. Don't oversalt."[50] The recipe that precedes it in the *Guter spise* is entitled *Hunre von Kriechen* ("Greek Chicken"): at this point a copyist reading the French *Rys en gresse* may well have understood *Rys en Grece*.

The *Vivendier* recipe is in any case not unique. It bears some resemblance to Recipe 71 in the *Viandier* which is for a dish whose earliest known name in that collection was simply *Ris*. In the Valais manuscript, however, the initial direction in this recipe is *Cuire en gresse*: "Cook in grease." Probably because of the use of saffron as a colorant in all *Viandier* versions of the dish, later copies change its name to *Ris engoullé* — whose English equivalent might be "Ruddy Rice". At Recipes 243 (*Aliter*) and 311, the *Menagier de Paris* has substantially the same sort of dish, along with a lean-day alternative that substitutes almond milk for the fat bouillon.

---

[50] Ed. Hans Hajek, *Das buch von guter spize. Aus der Würzburg-Münchener Handschrift* (Texte des späten Mittelalters, Heft 8), Berlin (Erich Schmidt), 1958, p. 16.

74 ❖ The *Vivendier* ❖

Cooking rice in a fat bouillon is otherwise not entirely unknown: see the *Cuoco napolitano*, Recipes 8 and 129, for instance.

❖ ❖ ❖ ❖ ❖ ❖ ❖ ❖

[51. Vermiseaux de cecille]

Vermiseaux de cecille sont fais de paste ossi petis comme petis vers qui se trouvent es fromaiges; et les font les petittez fillez du pais ou temps d'esté pour toutes saisons seschier au solloil pour mieulx garder; il les fault bien eslire et laver, puis mettre essuer comme dit est du rys, et cuire en bon boullon gras bien ensaffrenné; et du fin fromage gratté jetté au dreschier par dessus.

Sicilian Vermicelli are made of dough as fine as small worms that are found in cheese. Young country girls make them in summertime for the whole year, drying them in the sun to make them last longer. They should be well culled and washed, then set to dry as was said for the Rice[51]*, and cooked in good fat bouillon with a good lot of saffron; when dishing up, fine grated cheese sprinkled on top.*

This dish is remarkable for several reasons: the dishname retains the Italian form for the genre (*vermicelli*) — albeit with some inevitable frenchification; and the qualification of geographic provenance (*de Cecile*) acknowledges a recognition that this genre, or perhaps just this particular treatment of it, is of distant, rather exotic origin. Implicitly the recipe for Sicilian Vermicelli undertakes to retain the authenticity of this "foreign" dish.

Other occurrences of vermicelli are found only in Italian recipe collections. The only other reference to *pasta asciutta* from Sicily is in the Neapolitan Collection's *Macharoni ciciliani* (Recipe 15), echoed in Martino's Recipe 78 for *Maccaroni siciliani*.

❖ ❖ ❖ ❖ ❖ ❖ ❖ ❖

[52. Potee de poullaille]

Potee[52.1] **de poullaille: despechiez les par piecez et suffrisiez; puis prenez bon boullon, esve rose, gingembre, canelle, clou, graine, vin et vergus; faictez tout boullir ensamble, et vostre poullaille**[52.2] **avoecquez, une**[52.3] **onde.**

---

[51] That is, according to Recipe 50, before the fire.
[52.1] Above this word is written the word *potage* in smaller lettering.
[52.2] ms: *poull* with a superscript.
[52.3] ms: *une* is repeated.

Poultry Pottage. Cut them up into pieces and sautee them. Then get good bouillon, rosewater, ginger, cinnamon, cloves, grains of paradise, wine and verjuice; bring everything to a boil together, including your poultry.

This so-called *potee* is a remarkably commonplace preparation, as least as far as procedures are concerned. Even the meat is ordinary, undifferentiated "poultry". It is merely to be reduced to chunks, sauteed, and then boiled briefly in a seasoned bouillon. About the only noteworthy peculiarity in the recipe is the dish's use of rosewater (*esve rose*). Though fairly common in Italian and Catalan cookery, this ingredient is exceptional in French kitchens. The present recipe is the only one in the *Vivendier* that calls for rosewater.

The generic term *potee* is itself unusual. The scribe, or some subsequent user of the book, realized that the term might not be understood and has glossed it, in fine lettering above it, with the more universal word *potage*. This latter word is, in fact, the term identifying the genre of dish in the next recipe. The *FEW* (Vol. 9, p. 267a) gives as the earliest sense of the word *potée* "ce qu'on met dans un pot pour faire du potage," citing François Rabelais in the 1530s. The same entry provides a number of more modern, regional meanings which generally have to do with particular varieties of pottage: for instance, in *namurois* the word *potée* designates a "potage fait avec des morceaux de pain dans du café". Dictionaries of early French generally gloss *potee* as merely "potful" (*e.g.* T-L, 7, col. 1652). In the printed *Viandier* (as edited by Pichon and Vicaire) the term may have the acceptation of "a variety of preparation cooked in a pot": *Pour faire une potee de langue de beuf et de tetyne de vache* (p. 164); or merely the sense of "the contents of a pot": *... fais bouillir ta potee ... jusques ta dicte potee sera bien cuyte* (p. 206). Either sense may be understood in the Kassel manuscript.

❖   ❖   ❖   ❖   ❖   ❖   ❖   ❖

[53. Potage grenné]

[f. 162r (cxlviii)] **Potage grenné**[53] **: prenez pain gratuisié et le mettez boullir en bon boullon gras bien ensaffrenné; et quant il est bien cuit, prenez moyeux d'oes bien batus et fromage graté et, en fillant, sy jettez dedens en remuant dilligamment; faictez boullir une onde; puis dreschiez bien et chauldement, et pouldrez ou chucquerez par dessus, ou du fromage gracté.**

---

[53] ms: *grene*, with a nasal superscript.

Gravy Pottage. Get grated bread and set it to boil in good fat bouillon with a good lot of saffron. When it is well cooked, get well beaten egg yolks and grated cheese, and pour it in, in a slow, continuous stream, stirring attentively. Bring it to a boil. Then dish it up good and hot; sprinkle spice powder or sugar over top, or some grated cheese.

In Recipe 30, above, for *Une grenee fourmentee*, we found a dish or dish combination into which it seemed that a *grain* — some sort of meat — was to be incorporated. Now a *Potage grenné* seems to be a pottage *without* any meat whatsoever, even implied as an accompaniment. It may well be that, as with the early recipe for *Grenee fourmentee*, though the meat is not explicitly present, it may be understood to be there at the time the writer directs, *puis dreschiez bien et chauldement*: meat (of some sort) is being "dressed" carefully by the hot cheese-and-egg-yolk pottage. We may note that both the preceding and following recipes begin by sauteeing a meat, and then setting it aside while a sauce is composed.

❖ ❖ ❖ ❖ ❖ ❖ ❖ ❖

[54. Brouet de hongherie]

Brouet de hongherie : faictez grain suffrit tel que vous vouldrez ; prenez pain brullé bien roux, sang de cochon, d'oison ou aultre, deffait de bon boullon et passé parmy l'estamine, canelle, gingembre, clou et graine, macis et poivre long, vin, vergus et vin aigre, et faictez tout boullir ensamble, bien liant et de couleur sanguine ; jettez par dessus vostre grain chaudement.

Hungarian Broth. Sautee whatever meat you wish. Get toasted bread, the blood of a piglet, gosling or some other, distempered with good bouillon and strained, cinnamon, ginger, cloves, grains of paradise, mace and long pepper, wine, verjuice and vinegar, and boil everything together so that it is very thick and the colour of blood. Pour it hot over your meat.

The four recipes that conclude this section of the compilation mark a distinct change from what has immediately preceded. These four recipes all have something of the unusual about them. Whether because of an ingredient or a procedure, or the suggestion of an exotic origin, the dishes they represent do not seem to be standard, everyday preparations that the cook or author who earlier relied on the *Viandier*'s fourteenth-century staples might turn to very often. Perhaps not surprisingly, the names of several of these four recipes sound as if they might have become a little garbled in either oral or written transmission; the cooks or scribes may not have recognized the non-traditional dishnames here.

The name Hungarian Broth is, like Sicilian Vermicelli (Recipe 51, above), an acknowledgement — perhaps with some little pretentiousness — that this dish is exotic. In other recipe collections the kingdom of Hungary seems noteworthy only for its torts: in Bockenheim (Recipe 37) a *Torta pro Ungaris et Bohemis*; in the Venetian collection (Recipe 113), *Torta ungaresca*; and in the *Buone vivande* (Recipe 2), *Torta unganesca*. The one obvious exotic quality that the *Vivendier*'s particular "Hungarian" dish possesses lies in its dark russet hue, a colour which the recipe identifies as being "of blood". This quality does not relate our broth to the Hungarian torts elsewhere. To produce this colour, which appears to constitute an essence of the dish here, the various colours of the toast, blood, wine, verjuice and vinegar will all tend to make their contributions.

With a good range of six spices — including long pepper — the flavour of the Hungarian Broth is also distinctly rich.

❖ ❖ ❖ ❖ ❖ ❖ ❖ ❖

[55. La brehee]

La brehee : prenez ognons pellez et decoppez bien menus, pouris de cuire, puis suffris en beau sain de lard ; faictez[55.1] vostre grain d'oyez saleez, de porc, ou aultrez salures ; prenez amandes pelleez bien broyeez, deffaictez de bon boullon ou de puree de pois, gingembre, canelle, poivre noir ;[55.2] et chucquere largement au dreschier pouldrez par dessus. En[55.3] cas pareil se fait de blans poreaulx sans espices.

The Brehee. Get onions, peeled, finely chopped, boiled until disintegrating, and sauteed in good rendered lard. Do your salted goose meat, or salt pork or any other salted meat. Get well ground peeled almonds, distempered with good bouillon or with pea puree, ginger, cinnamon and black pepper. On dishing it up, sugar sprinkled generously over top.

In a similar way the dish is made with white leeks, without spices.

[55.1] A verb may be missing here: since the recipe contains no direction how the meat is to be prepared or cooked, and since the meats listed are all expressly of the salted, preserved sort, a missing verb might be *boullir*. However, it is not unknown for a late-medieval French recipe to use the verb *faire* is the sense of "to cook".

[55.2] The rubricator has inserted a punctuation slash before and after the phrase *et chucquere*; there is no subsequent punctuation until after *par dessus*. The punctuation here should likely indicate that sugar alone is the serving garnish, sprinkled on top of the onion, almond milk and spice sauce.

[55.3] The rubricator has put red strokes on the capital *E* as if marking the beginning of a distinct recipe or variation of a recipe.

La Brehee is unknown as a dishname elsewhere in medieval cookery. Its meaning is not immediately obvious. Several possible interpretations exist, of which the most likely has to do with the action of grinding or crushing. Godefroy (1, 739b) indicates that *broie* (*braie*) was either a kneading-trough or a pestle; verbal derivatives of these forms of that noun, *broiier* and *braiier*, were early forms of the modern French *broyer*, "to pound, crush, grind, pulverize".[55.4] However, the obvious difficulty with such an etymology is that nothing significant or substantial in this preparation, neither the onions nor the meat, is in fact expressly "ground." Though it is true that the almonds are to be pulverized (*bien broyeez*) and reduced to milk, this procedure is entirely normal and couldn't possibly be reason for the dish's name.

For the principal ingredient, the salt meat (whether of goose, pork, or other), the single, simple direction "do your meat" (*faictez vostre grain*) seems a little inadequate, either as an explicit culinary direction or in defence of the suggested interpretation of the dishname. It is very tempting to imagine that the scribe is at fault here, that he should have written something like *faictes boullir vostre grain ... et le broyez ...* : "boil your meat ... and grind it up ... ," or even simply *faictes breher/broyer vostre grain*. In that case the name of the dish would reflect that this was a preparation of meat paste, of much the same *genre* as the dish called *Mortereul* in other recipe collections.[55.5]

No other known prepared dish seems to combine salt fowl or meat with chopped, sauteed onions, almond milk, spices and sugar, whether this last is a garnish or not. However, the variant mentioned in the final sentence of this recipe was commonly prepared. Both the *Menagier* and Chiquart's *Du fait de cuisine* tell how to make up, without spices, a very similar dish which was called, simply, White Leeks.[55.6]

[55.4] The form *breez* of this verb is attested (repeatedly) in the *Enseignements*, a collection in which Carole Lambert has found a good number of Norman dialectal traits (in her *Trois réceptaires culinaires médiévaux*, pp. 30–31). In English recipes of the time the usual verb with an equivalent sense is "to bray".

[55.5] Thus in the *Menagier* at Recipe 236; other versions of this ground meat dish — its name derived from the word for "mortar" — turn up quite broadly in Latin, Italian, Catalan and English collections.

[55.6] At Recipe 50 and Recipe 16, respectively. The *Menagier*'s directions for this dish read as follows:
Poree Blanche est dicte ainsi pource qu'elle est faicte du blanc des poreaulx, a l'eschine, a l'andoulle et au jambon, es saisons d'amptonne et d'iver a jour de char. ... Et premierement l'en eslit, mince, lave et esverde les poreaulx — c'est assavoir en esté quant iceulx poreaulx sont jeunes, maiz en yver quant iceulx poreaulx sont plus vielz et plus durs, il les couvient pourboulir en lieu d'esverder.

[56. Pignagoscé sur chapons]

[f. 162v] Ung pignagoscé sur chapons: bien cuis en bon boullon, decopez par lopins, puis suffris en beau sain de lard; prenez les foyez de vos chapons et les broyez tresbien, puis prenez pain harlé, tempré en bon vergus, tout passé parmy l'estamine, gingembre, clou, graine, deffait de vin rouge et de vin aigre; faictez tout boullir ensamble; et du persin effueillié; jettez par dessus vostre grain chaudement.

A Pignagoscé on Capons. [*The capons are*] *well cooked in good bouillon, cut up into chunks, then sauteed in good rendered lard. Get the livers of your capons and grind them up well; then get toast, tempered in good verjuice, everything strained, ginger, cloves, grains of paradise, distempered with red wine and vinegar. Boil everything together, along with some parsley leaves. Pour it hot over your meat.*

As with the previous recipe, the name of this dish poses a problem: what does *ung pignagosce* or *pignagoscé* mean? The term, whether word or dishname, is unknown in any glossary or in other recipe collection of this period. If we were to guess at a meaning for this *pignagoscé*, we might try to break the word into parts: *pigne*, a "pine" or, more particularly, "pine-cone" and *agoscé*, a variant form of *angoscier* and *angoissier*, "to vex, afflict, fill with anguish."[56] In any case, whatever the meaning of its name, this is a hot, dark, rather thick and vinegary serving sauce composed of spices, wine, vinegar and parsley, and thickened with strained chicken liver and bread. Served on sauteed chunks of capon, this reddish-brown sauce, containing bits of green parsley, might indeed make the garnished dish look like "anguished pine-cones."

... *Et aussi cuire des ongnons mincez, puis frire les ongnons. Et aprés, frire iceulx poireaulx avec les ongnons qui ja sont fris, puis mectre tout cuire en un pot. Et du lait de vasche se c'est en Charnage; et a jour de poisson et se c'est en Karesme, l'en y met lait d'amandes. Et se c'est a jour de char, quant iceulx poreaulx d'esté sont esverdez, ou les poreaulx d'iver pourbouliz, comme dit est, l'en les met en ung pot cuire en l'eaue des salures, ou du porc, et du lart dedens.* ...

Given that this dish is feasible in the winter, the pork loin, sausage and ham with which the cook begins would all be salted — the *salures* mentioned toward the end.

[56] Another guess might begin with the noun *pignate*, a variant form of *peignate* (Godefroy, 6, 60c), whose sense is a (copper) stew pot or cauldron, and, by extension, the stew cooked in this vessel; and the qualification *gossé* (Godefroy, 4, 316b), glossed as *cossu* or "rich".

[57. Lyemesolles sur tout bon grain ...]

Lyemesolles sur tout bon grain, cochon ou aultre: decoppé[57.1] par lopins et cuit en bon boullon, puis mis essuer sur une belle nape; prenez mie de pain blancq tempré en vergus, et moyeulx d'oes, tout passé parmy l'estamine, saffren, gingembre, clou, graine et poivre long, deffait de vin et de vin aigre; faictez tout boullir ensamble; et mettez vostre grain en plas[57.2], jettez pardessus.

Snails, on any good meat, piglet or other. The meat is cut up into chunks and cooked in good bouillon, then set to dry on a clean cloth. Get white bread crumbs tempered in verjuice, and egg yolks, everything strained, saffron, ginger, cloves, grains of paradise and long pepper, distempered with wine and vinegar. Boil everything together. Set out your meat in platters, pour [the sauce] over top.

This is not a dish of or for snails, but rather a dish in which the meat, cut into small *lopins* and covered with a smooth, brownish yellow sauce, takes on something of the humped appearance of snails.

Snails were not themselves a common foodstuff in late-medieval cookery. Dr. Jacques Despars, as interested in foods as any physician of this time, noted with surprise the consumption of snails in Aragon and Catalonia.[57.3] They are seen as the principal element in a prepared dish described by the *Menagier de Paris*. His paragraph devoted to snails follows an equally unexpected one on frogs. As usual, however, he is concerned as much with the manner of obtaining the best snails — which the reader, presumably, will be doing himself or herself — as with describing how they are to cleaned, cooked and presented.[57.4] The final comment of the bourgeois author about snails, that "they are for wealthy people," is noteworthy. Given that the *Menagier* apparently had the means to eat virtually as well as his monarch, his comment seems to indicate that in the French gastronomy of the time snails were

---

[57.1] Both of the words *decoppé* and, later, *cuit* are in the masculine singular, and seemingly agree with the word *grain* rather than with *lyemesolles*.

[57.2] ms.: *emplas*.

[57.3] See Jacquart, "Le regard d'un médecin," p. 50.

[57.4] "*Lymassons*, that are called *escargolz*. They should be taken in the morning. Pick the young, small ones with black shells, from vine or elder leaves. Then wash them repeatedly until they give off no more foam, and once again in salt and vinegar; cook them in water. Then you should draw them from their shell with the tip of a pin or needle; then remove their tail, which is black (for that is their excrement), wash them, cook them in boiling water. Then take them out, set them on a plate or in a bowl to eat with bread. Some people say they are better fried with onions, in oil or some other liquid, after being cooked as above. They are eaten with spice powder. They are for wealthy people." *Menagier de Paris*, Recipe 257.

rare and that their consumption was limited to a very prescribed economic elite. In the Neapolitan Collection (Recipe 161), also, and in the *De honesta voluptate* of Platina (Recipe IX,39), snails are prepared (by boiling or frying, according to their size), then dressed and eaten as the major ingredient in a dish.

❖ ❖ ❖ ❖ ❖ ❖ ❖ ❖

[58. A faire .i. poullet aler rosti sur le table]

A faire .i. poullet aler rosti sur le table: preng ung poullet ou aultre oisiel tel qu'il te plaira, sy le plume tout vif a l'eaue chaude tresnettement; puis preng lez moioeufs de .ii. ou .iii. oeufs, et soient bastus avoecq pouldre de saffren et fleur de ble, et destemprés d'eaue crasse ou de la craisse qui[58.1] chiet soubz le rost en la paiele saininoire; et de [f. 163r (cxlix)] ceste mistion, a tout une plume, dore et pains tresbien ton poullet tant qu'il ait coulleur pareille a viande rostie; et, ce fait, quant on vouldra servir a table, mettez la teste du poulet dessoulz son elle, et le tourne entre tes mains et le touppie tant qu'il soit bien endormis; puis l'asiies[58.2] sur ton plat avoecq l'autre rot, et quant on le vaura trenchier il se esveillera et s'en fuira par la table et abatra pos et hanaps, etc.

To make a Chicken be Served Roasted. Get a chicken or any other bird you want, and pluck it alive cleanly in hot water. Then get the yolks of 2 or 3 eggs; they should be beaten with powdered saffron and wheat flour, and distempered with fat broth or with the grease that drips under a roast into the dripping pan. By means of a feather glaze[58.3] and paint your pullet carefully with this mixture so that its colour looks like roast meat. With this done, and when it is about to be served to the table, put the chicken's head under its wing, and turn it in your hands, rotating it[58.4] until it is fast asleep. Then set it down on your platter with the other roast meat. When it is about to be carved it will wake up and make off down the table upsetting jugs, goblets and whatnot.

[58.1] ms.: *qui* repeated.

[58.2] For the scribe's *lasiies* two interpretations seem most possible: a form of *laissier*, "to leave", or of *asseoir*, "to seat" or "to set". Although a single *s* is not unknown with *laissier* (or *lasier*), the absence of an object weakens the case a little for that verb.

[58.3] Properly, *dorer* is "to gild" as with the rich reddish yellow of the egg yolks and saffron.

[58.4] The literal sense of the verb *topier* is closer to the movement of a top, "to twirl" or "to spin". This does seem rather a violent means to achieve the purpose, unless, perhaps, it is the person holding the fowl who is to whirl about. On the whole it would seem that stroking or petting the bird might be a more effective way to put it to sleep.

The *Vivendier*

With this recipe the collection once again changes its character. Here, however, there is not merely evidence of a different sort of recipe; the book is clearly composed of a several appended sets of disparate recipes, just as the last four recipes above represent a slightly different cuisine. What we also find at this point is a change of scribal hand as well, a change of terminology, a change of spellings, a change of prose style and, most significantly, several new ingredients unused in previous recipes. The compilation is continuing to grow by accretion, little by little, but now with a different writer, perhaps a different owner of these pages that will be bound in the manuscript — and, once more, with a different source for the recipes.

Although not entirely consistently, the new scribe now prefers to couch his instructions in the second person *singular* rather than the formal *vous* that we have seen up to this point, with *tes mains* and *ton plat* as confirmation in the present recipe. In all likelihood he is in this merely reproducing the style of his source. After two or three recipes this singular imperative will tend to shift hesitantly back to a formal plural. We may note the instruction *mettez la teste* curiously isolated in the middle of this *entremets*.

Up to this point in the manuscript, the scribe has been remarkably successful in spacing his recipes such that a text is not split over two pages. Previously only Recipe 42 was incomplete on the page on which the recipe began, with its final two lines having to be carried over to the top of f° 160v. The present scribe seems more concerned with squeezing his copy into whatever space is available. At the foot of this f° 163r he will find, in fact, that he has no space to conclude his copy.

This recipe bears no real "dishname", merely an imperfect description of what the recipe will enable the cook to do: the title misses the point, because the *apparently* roasted fowl is served *alive!* There is no real dishname perhaps for the very reason that there is no dish. In the best tradition of the *entremets*, this is a pretend preparation, and the simulation is that there is a roast chicken ("or other fowl you wish") ready to be eaten. The revelation of the real nature of this serving, the undeception of the table guests, is made all the more delightfully dramatic at the very last possible moment; the writer even anticipates the general glee sparked by the bird's most lively — indeed vigourous — escape from the carving knife.

❖ ❖ ❖ ❖ ❖ ❖ ❖ ❖

[59. A faire chanter ledit poullet mort ...]

A faire chanter ledit poullet mort et rosti, en la broque ou ens ou plat: preng le gosier de ton poullet et le loie a .i. bout et l'empli de vif argent et de souffre bastu, et continue tant qu'il soit plain a demy pauch prez; puis loye l'autre bout, no pas trop fort; et quant tu veulx qu'il chante, si mes⁵⁹ ton gosier ou poullet, tandis qu'il est bien chault, et quant les mistions s'eschaufferont, l'air qui cuidra yssir fera le son du poullet. Et ainsy fait on d'un oyson, d'un pourchellet et de tous aultrez oysiaulz. Et s'il ne sonne assés hault, si loye lez .ii. bous plus fort.

To Make that Chicken Sing when it is dead and roasted, whether on the spit or in the platter. Take the neck of your chicken and bind it at one end and fill it with quicksilver and ground sulphur, filling until it is roughly half full; then bind the other end, but not too tightly. When you want it to sing, [heat] your neck or chicken. When it is quite hot, and when the mixture heats up, the air that is trying to escape will make the chicken's sound. The same can be done with a gosling, with a piglet and with any other birds. And if it doesn't cry loudly enough, tie the two ends more tightly.

This *entremets* is a technical tour de force of which the writer seems confidently proud. While the trick of having a dead (and cooked) animal breathe fire is almost a commonplace in other fifteenth-century recipe collections — and, of course, see the *Vivendier*'s own version of this phenomenon in Recipe 15, above — nowhere in any other collection across Europe do we find a dead (and cooked) creature singing! Our author might himself crow at having produced such a unique wonder. To extract by these means a melodious squawk or squeal from a piglet, as a variant that the recipe suggests, would indeed present marvellous entertainment.

❖   ❖   ❖   ❖   ❖   ❖   ❖   ❖

[60. Un poisson ou une pieche de char ...]

A faire un poisson ou une pieche de char sans rompre, que une partie soit rostie, l'autre boullie, et l'aultre frite a l'oille ou au bure : pren des estoupes⁶⁰ ...   [incomplete]

To make a fish or a piece of meat, without dividing it, one part to be roasted, another boiled and the remainder fried in oil or butter. Get some tow ....

---

⁵⁹ Some text may be missing in this passage: perhaps *mes sur le feu*, or *mes s'eschauffer*. The punctuation slash that the scribe has inserted previous to the word *tandis* may also be stronger than a mere modern comma.

⁶⁰ *estoupes*: the *t* and the *u* are by no means certain, although *estoupes* certainly makes sense. The *Französisches Etymologisches Wörterbuch* (Vol. 12, p. 314b) glosses this word in Old French as "*partie la plus grossière de la filasse de chanvre*"; according to the same work the word derives from *stuppa*, glossed in German as *werg* or "tow".

84 ❖ The *Vivendier* ❖

🖋 The recipe is copied to the end of the last line on this folio, 163r; the top of the verso bears the beginning of another recipe. The compiler of the collection, or the scribe, may have broken off his copy of this recipe as he realized that a similar three-in-one trick had already been described earlier for the fish of Recipe 15. This beginning seems to promise to show how a piece of meat can be handled in a similar way. In any case, once again, the top of f° 163v. will begin another, distinct series of recipes.

❖ ❖ ❖ ❖ ❖ ❖ ❖ ❖

[61. Blanque sause non boulie ... a poissons]

[f. 163v] Pour faire blanque sause non boulie[61.1] appartenant a cabillaut, a escliffins, a rocques et pluseurs aultrez poissons.[61.2]

Prenés du pain blancq tailliés par lesques et le metés temprer en yauwe de bouillon et verius[61.3] ; prendés des amandes une .xx.aine et les estampés, et puis le pain bruyerés avoecq lesdites amandes, et passés parmy l'estamine desmellé de verius et ung petit de vinaigre ; et quant ladite sause est faitte, prenés poudre de blancq gengembre a quantitet pour la savourer ; qu'elle ne soit point trop forte.

Item, ladite sause sert pareillement quant on voelt qu'elle soit gaune pour rocques ou aultre poisson ou gaune sause appartient : prenés vostre pain et le tostés tant qu'il soit .i. petit rousset et le passés en le maniere comme dessus, et mettés gaune poudre ensafrenee ; et se ladite poure ne gaunist assés, prenés .i. petit de saffran.

Item[61.4] : pareillement quant vous volés qu'elle soit verde, prendés brun pain tempret en vertius, .i. petit[61.5] rosti ausi, et estampés

---

[61.1] ms.: the words *non boulie* are inserted above the line by means of a carat.

[61.2] Exceptionally, this *incipit* constitutes a rubric for its recipe. It is indented and slightly separated from the paragraph that follows. The recipe itself, like the next one, is rationally and clearly subdivided into paragraphs, each announced in the margin by a "paragraph" sign (¶) for which the new scribe has a noticeable predilection.

[61.3] ms.: *et verius* is added in the left margin. A mark following the word *bouillon* indicates the proper position of the phrase in the text.

[61.4] This paragraph seems to have been inserted, with its lines somewhat squeezed together, into the space originally left between Recipes 61 and 62.

[61.5] ms.: between *petit* and *rosti*, the words *le pain*, although not really necessary, are inserted above the line by means of a caret.

❖ II. Text, Translation & Commentary ❖   85

tresbien vostre ozelle ou aultre vert seloncq le tamps avoecq le pain et mettre de le poure de gengembre ou autre fine poure.[61.6]

Et[61.7] qui veolt faire les dites sause sentir les aux, tant a le blanque comme a le verde, se le viande le requiert, on en puelt estamper avoecq le pain; et a ce ne convient point de poure.

To make Unboiled White Sauce suitable for cod, haddock, roach and several other fish. Get slices of white bread and set them to temper in bouillon and verjuice; get a dozen almonds and pound them and then grind up the bread with the almonds and strain this, mixed with verjuice and a little vinegar. When that sauce is made, get enough powder of white ginger to flavour it; it should not be too strong.

Also. That sauce is likewise useful when a yellow sauce is needed for roach or any other fish for which a yellow sauce is suitable. Get your bread and toast it until it is a little rusty coloured and strain it as above; and add in yellow, saffroned powder; and if that powder doesn't give enough yellow, get a little saffron.

Also. Similarly, when you want it to be green. Get brown bread tempered in verjuice, a little toasted, too. Grind your sorrel, or other green colourant depending on the season, along with the bread; and add in powdered ginger or some other fine spice powder.

Should anyone wish to give a garlic flavour to those sauces, to both the white version and the green, if the meat calls for it, [garlic] can be crushed with the bread. There should be no spice powder in this case.

The new series of recipes that begins at the top of f° 163v. is surprisingly commonplace in nature — particularly after our flights of fancy with roasted birds that up and flutter away, and chickens and piglets that sing before their own supper. The first of these is a sauce, with variations on its, for specific sorts of fish. The basic sauce here is the only one to which the recipe's name, *Blanque sause*, can properly apply: it is a mild ginger sauce whose fundamental ingredient is almond

---

[61.6] This is the last paragraph of this recipe as it was copied. As was mentioned in a previous footnote, this paragraph seems to have been a later insertion. Between this recipe and the next one, Recipe 62, however, the scribe has drawn an insertion mark. A second insertion mark that corresponds to it is found at the foot of the facing page, f° 164r, and precedes the paragraph which is appended here. The first word of that paragraph, *et*, does not have a capital letter, although it does have before it the scribe's conventional paragraph sign to indicate that what follows does constitute a distinct paragraph.

[61.7] Clearly at the point where the scribe squeezed the previous paragraph between Recipes 61 and 62 there was insufficient space for this present paragraph as well. He used an insertion mark to place it at the foot of the facing folio, 164r, where 2 cm of space was available after Recipe 65.

milk and which uses only clear or white ingredients such as white bread (untoasted) and (expressly) white ginger.

The three variations on the basic White Sauce involve modifications in colour and flavour. The first requires light-brown toast as the thickener and *gaune poudre ensafrenee*, by which the author may intend either the ginger powder already mentioned earlier, or a mixture of common spices which this book has referred to in other recipes as simply "powder"; in either case saffron is to be added in order to ensure the appropriate yellow hue. The second variant uses a slightly toasted dark bread (rather than white bread) along with sorrel or some other green colourant. Ground sorrel was occasionally used as a source of green in French cookery. The fifteenth-century Vatican copy of the *Viandier* (Recipe 170) sets out a list of ingredients that could be relied upon to lend such a green to a prepared dish: parsley, herb bennet, sorrel, vine leaves or vine shoots, gooseberries and, in winter, new wheat sprouts. The conditional phrase, "according to the season," recognizes that, at the time of year the cook is preparing this dish, fresh green sorrel may not be available in the kitchen garden; in that case the cook will have to have recourse to some other green colourant. The final variant provides for a garlic flavour in either of two preceding coloured sauces.

The limited range of fish for which these sauces are specific is surprising. Cod, haddock and roach alone are named; the first two are sea-fish, the third is a fresh-water fish. Only the rather vague, blanket application of the Unboiled White Sauce to *pluseurs aultrez poissons*, and the Yellow Sauce to *aultre poisson ou gaune sause appartient*, accords some more general usefulness to these preparations.

Again we observe that the scribe's style is slightly more formal, using the second person plural *vous*. What is most striking here is that this recipe seems not to have been copied wholesale from some source. Rather it has been compiled, and rather awkwardly, over time, and may well derive from the writer's own experience.

A White Sauce is known in other recipe collections of the late Middle Ages. The *Forme of Cury* contains a *Sawse blaunche* (Recipe 140); while its primary ingredients are the same (almond milk, verjuice and ginger), this English version is intended for use with boiled capons. In the *Recueil de Riom* (Recipe 41) a *Saulse blanche* is made with bread, verjuice and ground white ginger.

❖   ❖   ❖   ❖   ❖   ❖   ❖   ❖

[62. Bouruet sur ung cappon rosti]

Pour faire ung bouruet[62.1] sur ung cappon rosti : prendés du verius et

---

[62.1] The initial letter of this word appears to have been written with some hesitation, perhaps first as a *v* and then modified to a *b*. The upper flourish of the *b* is detached from the lower part of the letter.

.ii. mieulx d'oef crut sans les glaires, et le moitiet du foye du cappon, et le passer parmy une estamine[62.2]; et puis prendre de le poudre de gengembre et du persin hechiet bien menut et le cuire tout en samble en une payelle; et puis le jetter sur le cappon en .i. plat, et mettre des souppes a maniere de tostees ens ou plat.

Et[62.3] pareillement sur becquet ser ladite sause; et se le verius estoit trop picquant, fuist a l'un ou a l'autre, il convient prendre ung bien peu d'yawe de buillon.

To make a Bouruet on a Roast Capon. Get verjuice, two raw egg yolks without the whites, and half of the capon's liver; strain it. Then get ground ginger and very finely chopped parsley, and cook everything together in a pan; then pour it over the capon on a platter. Set out [toasted] sops within the platter [cut] after the fashion of pieces of toast.

Likewise serve this sauce over pike. And if the verjuice is too sharp, whether on the first dish or the second, you should add in a very little bouillon.

The preparation that appears here to be called a *bouruet* (or perhaps *bourvet* or *bournet*) is unknown with exactly that spelling in any other recipe collection. The dish consists basically of a meat (here either capon or pike) with (toasted) sops beneath and a tangy sauce over both.

These *tostees* garnishing the platter serve to sop up any excess sauce. As the text suggests, they are standard preparations. On two occasions the *Viandier* points to their nature. In Recipe 54, for River Mallard, where one manuscript version calls for the duck to be set on *tostees de pain*, another specifies *souppes longuetes, tenves, brullees*: "elongated, thin, darkly toasted sops." In Recipe 198, for Gilded Toast, the dish reads, "Get hard white bread and slice it into squared *tostees* and toast them on the grill ... ." These *tostees* are merely thin squares of toast and function first as a decorative garnish and then as a sop; in the *Viandier*'s Recipe 198, they may be coated with egg yolk and deep fried.

An English recipe may represent a remote version of this dish. In his two collections, Austin has edited recipes for *Soppes pour Chamberleyne* and *Soupes Jamberlayne*[62.4] in which a sauce of wine and spices is poured over toasted sops. As these latter are to be prepared, the text reads: *Then take paynmain, and kutte hit in a maner of Browes, and tost hit, and ley hit in a dissh* ... . Our *bouruet*

[62.2] ms.: the word *estamine* has a (nasal?) slur over the letters *mi*.

[62.3] This word has no capital.

[62.4] At pp. 90 and 11, respectively. See above, the *Vivendier*'s Recipe 16.

could embody the same principle as the English "eyebrows" — that is, presumably, exceptionally thin, curved slices of toast, used as sops.[62.5]

❖ ❖ ❖ ❖ ❖ ❖ ❖ ❖

[63. Oes mirés a le sause]

Pour faire oes mirés a le sause : premiés faittes vos oef mirés et les retournés[63.1] ung a ung pour les chuyre a deux les, et puis les mettés en ung plat ; et en aprés prendés des[63.2] oygnons et le frissiés tresbien en bure, et puis les purer ; et prendés du pain rosti sans bruller et temprer en verius avoecq ung petit de vinaigre, et ce [f. 164r (cl)] passer avoec les ognons ; et puis le boullir tout ensamble[63.3] un petit ; et le gitter sur les oef.

To make Mirés Eggs in a Sauce. First make your Mirés Eggs and flip them over one by one to cook on both sides; then set them out on a platter. Then get onions and fry them well in butter, then drain them. Get unburnt toast, temper it in verjuice with a little vinegar, and strain this with the onions; then boil everything together a little. Pour it over the eggs.

The preparation itself is not complex; the eggs are simply cooked — whether poached or fried is not specified — and then they are dressed in a serving sauce. The dish remains standard in a modern cook's repertoire: eggs *au miroir*, the yolks prepared by baking to a glossy finish and then *nappés* with a cream sauce. Two centuries after the *Vivendier*, La Varenne and Pierre de Lune will use the modern term for this dish.[63.4] In both writers these are butter-fried eggs in which the yolk is not so cooked as to lose its yellow colour but, presumably, the white has been given a reflective gleam.

❖ ❖ ❖ ❖ ❖ ❖ ❖ ❖

[62.5] It may be noted in passing that in the recipe called *Schyconys with the bruesse* at p. 32 in Austin's edition the text instructs the cook to *kytte thin Brewes, and skalde hem with the same brothe*; then, on serving the chicken, to lay out the chicken *and ley uppe-on this browes*.

[63.1] ms.: *retones*, with a superscript abbreviation in the middle of the word.

[63.2] ms.: *deo*.

[63.3] ms.: *ensamble* added in the left margin.

[63.4] Pierre François de La Varenne, *Le cuisinier françois* (1651), ed. Jean-Louis Flandrin and Philip and Mary Hyman, Paris (Montalba), 1983, p. 254; Pierre de Lune, *Le cuisinier* (1656) in *L'art de la cuisine française au XVIIe siècle*, ed. Gilles and Laurence Laurendon, Paris (Payot), 1995.

[64. Potage de lievre]

Pour faire potage de lievre : prenés vo lievre et le fourboulés et lardés et le metés en rost ; et puis, quant il est rotis, faittes vo potage: prenés du pain et le fait tout noir au feu bien fort et le mettés tempré en[64.1] crase yauwe sans crasse ; et puis le passés et metés vergus et vin aigre ; et qui ne soit point fort de vin aigre forque le gout[64.2]; et puis metés menues espesses et ung pau de brun cuquere et puis le boullés ; et quant il est bouly, se coppés vo lievre par pieches et le mettés au pot ; et le laisiés demy eure devant[64.3] qui soit tamps de diner.[64.4]

To make Stewed Hare. Take your hare and parboil it, lard it and set it to roast. When it has roasted, make your pottage: get bread, blacken it over a very hot fire and set it to temper in greasy, fat-free stock, then strain it and add in verjuice and vinegar — and it should not be at all strong with vinegar but have only the flavour. Then add in minor spices and a little brown sugar, and boil it. When it has boiled, cut up your hare into pieces and put them into the pot; let it sit half an hour before it is dinner time.

This Hare Stew is interesting in part as an indication of the mediocre culinary level of these last recipes in the *Vivendier*, and in part of the commonplace nature of the main foodstuffs. Capons, sea-fish, eggs, chicks — these, and a hare, are not exotic or expensive ingredients out of which to prepare dishes; the household budgets where these recipes were normally prepared would not be strained. We might suspect that such budgets tended to be of rather modest dimensions to begin with. In dining halls where the *Vivendier*, and its sources, were of any practical help, exoticism in culinary matters seems to be limited to squawking chickens and a fish cooked in three different ways.

The specification of "brown" sugar is curious, though. To conclude his recipe for the variety of Cameline Sauce that is made at Tournai, the *Menagier de Paris* (Recipe 271) adds in *du succre roux*. In a note the editors of this text propose that the phrase here represents "sugar mixed with spice to give a reddish colour,"

[64.1] ms.: following the word *en*, a series of letters — apparently *crisauy* — have been stroked out.

[64.2] ms.: *gou*, followed by one of the rubricator's red punctuation marks. The word is spelled *gout* later at the same place in the subsequent version of this dish (Recipe 66).

[64.3] ms.: *de vant*.

[64.4] Following this word the rubricator has drawn a double stroke — exceptional in this series of recipes — seemingly marking the end of this recipe. After these two red strokes, in somewhat lighter ink, are the words *verte folium*: "turn over." The advice is sound: the second recipe for *Potage de lievre* is, indeed, at the top of the *verso* of this folio.

although this seems unlikely. Concerning a shipment of sugar purchased in England in 1443, Sidney Mintz writes that some sugar was

> more refined ('kute' — later, 'cute,' from the French *cuit*) than the rest. Less refined brown sugar, partially cleaned and crystallized, was imported in chests — the 'casson sugar,' later called 'cassonade,' one finds in the inventory lists of grocers in the mid-fifteenth century. This sugar could be refined further, but commercial refineries do not appear in England for another century.[64.5]

A pure, highly-refined white sugar, normally available in powdered form, was universally recognized as being the preferable grade. We can only speculate that our author's specification of brown sugar in this recipe must be intended primarily as a measure of economy.

❖   ❖   ❖   ❖   ❖   ❖   ❖   ❖

[65. Pastés de pouchins]

Pour faire pastés de pouchins: metés ens ou pastés sur le fons ung lit de lart de porcq, et pareillement sur les pouchins; et quant[65.1] **le pasté sera kuys, prendés une escuelle de verius et .ii. mieulx d'oex durs kuit, avoecq une dousainne d'amande — les peller et estamper — et puis desmeller**[65.2] **ses amandes avoecq lez oex dessusdits et le verius, et passer parmy l'estamine et le mettre boulir avoecq ung peu de burre le grandeur d'une nois; et quant il est bouli, prendre de le poure de gengembre ce que besoing est, et tout caut getter ens ou pasté par deseure.**

To make Chick Pies. Put into the pastry shell, on its bottom, a layer of pork lard, and likewise over the chicks. When the pie is baked, get a bowlful of verjuice and two hard-boiled egg yolks, then a dozen almonds — peel and grind them, then mix these almonds in with the eggs and the verjuice, strain this and set it to boil with an amount of butter the size of a walnut. When it has boiled, add in a suitable amount of ginger powder, and pour the mixture hot through the top of the pie.

The recipe does not specify whether the Chick Pie is to be double-crusted, although this is certainly much more common. If the pie does indeed take an

---

[64.5] Sidney W. Mintz, *Sweetness and Power. The Place of Sugar in Modern History*, New York (Viking), 1985, p. 83.
[65.1] ms.: between *et* and *le* the word *quant* is inserted above the line by means of a carat.
[65.2] ms.: *des meller*.

upper crust, then the recipe is not entirely explicit in another regard. The preparation of a double-crusted pie would normally utilize a regular procedure for adding the "sauce" to the pie's main ingredient. Elsewhere, particularly in Italian recipe collections of this century, the cook is directed to make a hole in the upper crust *before* it is put into the oven; then, just as or just before the pie has finished baking (here: *quant le pasté sera finis*) a flavouring sauce is poured into the pie through that hole. The purpose behind this quite common last-minute addition was to retain all of the potential savour that the sauce mixture possessed without having any of it dissipated by evaporating out of the pie as it baked. In the next recipe the author makes up a little for his silence here on this standard procedure.

❖ ❖ ❖ ❖ ❖ ❖ ❖ ❖

[66. Potage de lievre]

[f. 164v] **Pour faire potage de lievre:** prenés vo lievre et le lardés tresbien sans le fourboulir ne devant ne aprés, et le metés rostir, et souvent arosser de sain de lart — et quant il est fondu, y mettre .i. peu de vinaigre; et ens, ou lieu de sain de lart, on peult mettre du sain d'auwe douch.

Pour faire ledit Potage: prenés du pain et le rostissiés bien noir, et incontinent le boutés en yauwe froide et le sachiés hors hastivement, tant seulement pour hoster la fumee du brulé; puis metés temprer en yauw[66.1] de buillon de char fresche ou[66.2] en verius et du vin vermeille, et passés parmy l'estamine vostre pain, et au passer deffaittes de vierius[66.3] et de vin, et du vin aigre pour[66.4] le donner gout — non point trop fort de vin esgre; et puis prendés vos especes a quantité — est assavoir du gengembre, des menues espices, et otant de canelle comme des deux aultres, avoecq ung peu de claux de ginofle qui voelt; et mettés lesdites espices en vostre brouuet quant il est passé, et fait boullir tout en samble en une payelle de fer ou de terre; et y mettés du sain de quoy vostre lievre ara estet aroset le quantité de .iiii. ou .v. petittes louchiés; et faittes tout boulir en samble, bien agouté de vinaigre et salé apoint; et ne soit point trop espés; et quant vostre brouuet sera bien boulit, mettés dessus vostre lievre, ou aultre char

---

[66.1] ms.: *sic*.
[66.2] The words *en yauw de buillon de char fresche ou* have been added in the left margin. A stroke from the last letter leads to the *en* of *en verius*.
[66.3] *sic*.
[66.4] ms.: the abbreviation is for the word *par*.

qui voelt, coppé par morsiaux, vostre lievre ou aultre char, ou tout entier; et en servés quant il vous plaist. Et sert la dite sause en pastés comme sause chaude, mais il fault la dite sause mettre ou pasté et puis le remettre en[66.5] ou four demy heure ou environ. Et sert as oysiaux de riviere et a pluseurs aultre chose.

Item: et pour faire deux plas de sause, vous poés prendre une pinte et demye de vin vermeille, une pinte de verius, et .i. petit de vinaigre, seloncq sa forche.

To make Stewed Hare. Get your hare and lard it well without parboiling it either before or after, and set it to roast, basting it often with rendered lard — when this has melted, add a little vinegar to it. Instead of rendered lard you can use rendered fresh goose grease.

To make that Stew. Get bread and toast it quite dark, then right away plunge it into cold water and pull it right out again, simply to do away with the burnt smell. Then set it to temper in fresh meat bouillon or in verjuice and some red wine; strain your bread, and when straining it distemper it with verjuice and wine, with some vinegar to flavour it, though not too strong with the vinegar. Then get your spices in quantity — that is, ginger, minor spices[66.6], and as much cinnamon as of the other two, with a few cloves should anyone wish; put those spices into your broth when it is strained. Boil everything together in an iron or earthenware pan, adding in 4 or 5 small spoonfuls of the lard with which the hare was basted; boil everything together, flavoured well with vinegar and salted as necessary. It should not be too thick. When your broth has boiled well, pour it over your hare, or over some other meat should you wish, whether cut up into pieces or whole. Serve it when you wish.

This sauce can be used in pasties like a Hot Sauce, but you have to put it in the pasty and then put the pasty back into the oven for half an hour or thereabouts. It can be used for river birds and for several other things.

Also, to make two platters of sauce you can get a pint and a half of red wine, a pint of verjuice and a little vinegar, depending on its strength.

The identity of name on both this recipe and Recipe 64 merely underscores the disagreements between them. While copying them from two clearly different sources, each with its own concept of the dish and of its preparation, our compiler has not bothered to modify the name that each source shows.

[66.5] *sic.*

[66.6] These *menues espices* are a mixture of the less common spices. The *Viandier* lists them in Recipe 191 as *grainne de paradiz, girofle et poivre long*: "grains of paradise, cloves and long pepper." In the next phrase, however, our text makes cloves an optional addition.

The main part of each recipe is in two parts: the preparation and cooking of the hare, and the preparation of the sauce, or stew, in which the meat is to be served. The preparation of the hare itself is different in the two versions, the first insisting on an initial parboiling, while the second emphasizes that no parboiling, *ne devant ne aprés*, is necessary. A basting compound in the second case adds moisture and flavour.

The nature of the sauce — the *potage* — is not only somewhat different but more detailed in this present version. Where previously a standard spice mixture flavours the hare sauce, it is now intended to be a fundamentally cinnamon sauce. And the author clarifies, among other things, the meaning of the earlier direction that this pottage needs little *de vinaigre forque le gout*. Then, too, in a certain sense Recipe 64 is also revisited here as the second source instructs how to use the *potage* in a pie (of, apparently, any sort of meat) by adding it through the crust when the pie is only partially baked.

As we have seen, the noting of precise quantities is not usual in this collection, nor in recipe collections generally at this time. The indications of amounts, even of relative amounts, that we find in this last recipe sets it somewhat apart from the usual late-medieval French practice.

❖

III. Ingredients and Glossary

A. Ingredients in the Recipes

Note: Variant spellings and plurals are indicated in parentheses.

meat (of unspecified animal): char (chars), grain, viande (viandes)
 (domestic): beuf, cochon, mouton, porc (porcq), pourchellet, vache
 (game): connir, lievre, lyemesolles, venoison
 (viscera and products): foye (foyez), sang
 (preserved meats): salures

fowl (unspecified): oisiel (oysiaulz, oysiaux)
 (domestic): auwe, chapon (cappon, chapons), oison (oyson), pouchins, poulet (poullet, poulez), poullaille
 (game): oysiaux (de riviere)

seafood (unspecified): poisson (poissons)
 (fish): anguille (anguilles, anguillez), becquet, brasmes, cabillaut, carpres, escliffins, esturgon, lamproye, luchs, menuyse, plais (plays), raye (rayes), rocques, solles, tenche (tenches), turbot
 (mollusks, crustaceans, etc.): crevesches

dairy products: bure (burre), cresme, fromage (fromaiges), lait de vache

eggs: oef (oeufs, oes, oels, oex, eulx), glaires, moyeulx (moyelx, moyeux, moioeufs, mioefz)

grains and their products: amidun (amigdun), ble, farine, fleur d'amidun, fleur de ble, fourment, pain, ris

vegetables and **herbs** (unspecificied): herbes
 (above ground): aux, bettez, cresson, espic (espicq), fevez, laurier, ozelle, persin, pois (poix), polioel, poreaulx, saille (sailles), sauge, silion, sourmetaine, ysope
 (below ground): ognons (oygnons)

spices, etc. (unspecified): espices (espicez, especes, espesses), poure (fine poure) canelle, clou (cloux, claux de ginofle), commin, garingal, gingembre (gengembre), graine (grains de paradis), macis, mughettes (mughettez, muscades), poivre (poivre long, poivre noir), saffren (saffran)

(sweeteners): chucquere (cuquere), dragié

fruits and **nuts**: amande (amandes, agmandes), chastaigne, orenge, pommes

liquids and **fats**:

(grape products): vin, vin rouge, vin vermeille, vergus (verius, vertius, vierius), vin (vin rouge, vin vermeille), vin aigre (vinaigre, vin esgre)

(other liquids): boullon (bouillon, buillon), esve (eaue, yauwe, yawe, yauw), esve rose, lait d'amandes, lait de vache

(fats): craisse (crasse, gresse), huille (oille), lard (lart), sain, sain de lard, sain d'auwe (douch)

B. Glossary of the Recipes

Resources

The following dictionaries and glossaries are cited partly for their authority in proposing the glosses here, and partly in order to indicate possible lexical relations. Each work is preceded by the *siglum* by which it is referred to in this Glossary.

A-N D: Louise W. Stone and William Rothwell, *Anglo-Norman Dictionary*, London (Modern Humanities Research Association), 1977–1992

Cotgrave: Randle Cotgrave, *A Dictionarie of the French and English Tongues*, London, 1611; repr. Columbia (University of South Carolina Press), 1950

Gamillscheg: Gamillscheg, *Etymologisches Wörterbuch der französischen Sprache*, Heidelberg (Carl Winter), 1928

FEW: Walther von Wartburg, *Französisches Etymologisches Wörterbuch*, Basel (Zbinden), from 1964

Godefroy: Frédéric Godefroy, *Dictionnaire de l'ancienne langue française et de tous ses dialectes du IXe au XVe siècles*, Paris (F. Vieweg), 1881–1902; repr. Vaduz (Kraus), 1965

Huguet: Edmond Huguet, *Dictionnaire de la langue française du seizième siècle*, Paris (Didier), 1925–67

Latham: R. E. Latham, *Dictionary of Medieval Latin from British Sources*, London (Oxford University Press), 1975–

Menagier: Baron Jérôme Pichon, ed., *Le Ménagier de Paris, traité de morale et d'économie domestique composé vers 1393 par un bourgeois parisien*, Paris (Société des Bibliophiles français), 1846

Pegolotti: Francesco Balducci Pegolotti, *La pratica della mercatura*. ed. Allan Evans, Cambridge, Mss. (Medieval Academy of America), 1936; repr. Vaduz (Kraus), 1970

REW: Wilhelm Meyer-Lübke, *Romanisches Etymologisches Wörterbuch*, Heidelberg (Carl Winter), 1911-[1920]

T-L: Adolf Tobler and Erhard Lommatzsch, *Altfranzösisches Wörterbuch*, Berlin (Weidmann), 1925– ; repr. and currently Wiesbaden (Steiner), 1955–

Words and numbers in **bold type** indicate the name of a recipe and its location in the collection.

Note that for the sake of simplicity and uniformity the English gloss may represent a verb by an infinitive, even where no infinitive form is attested in the French text.

affaittié 29: cleaned, eviscerated
agouté 66: flavoured
allemaigne 22: Germany; **Brouet d'allemaigne de char 22**
amande 65, amandes 14, 18, 20, 22, 28, 29, 50, 55, 61, 65, agmandes 12: almond
amidun 12, 30, amigdum 30: starch
Amplummus, un 17: apple sauce
anguille 28, 43, anguilles 2, 28, anguillez 2, 12: eel; **Assise d'anguillez 2**
argent 15, 59 silver; *cf.* argenteez 29: silvered, given a silver colour
assisse 2, 4: a serving, course; from *asseoir*, to set, set out (on a table); **Assise d'anguillez 2; ~ de venoison 4**
asur 15: azur, blue
auwe 66: goose; see also *oison* and *sain*, below
aux 33, 37, 38, 61: bot., *Allium sativum*, garlic (cloves of); **Aux blans 38, ~ camelins 37**
avoec 1, 10, 14, 22, 27, 40, 42, 45, 63, avoecq 16, 58, 61, 63, 65, avoeques 22, avoecques 46, avoecquez 20, 43, 52: with (*avec*)
barbe: see *Robert*, below
becquet 62: ichth., *Esox lucius*, pike; **Ung bouruet sur ung cappon rosti et ... becquet 62**; see also *luchs*, below

bettez 25: bot., *Beta vulgaris cicla*, beet greens, spinach beets, chard
beuf (boullon de) 25: beef
blans d'oes 8: egg whites; see also *glaires*
ble 30, 58: wheat
boucter 43, boutés 66: to thrust, dip (into a liquid)
boullon 19, 20, 21, 22, 23, 25, 27, 28, 29, 44, 45, 49, 50, 51, 52, 53, 54, 55, 56, 57, bouillon 61, buillon 62, 66: bouillon, water in which a foodstuff has boiled
bouruet 62: a variety of serving sauce (for roast capon or pike); **Ung bouruet sur ung cappon rosti et ... becquet 62**; the name may be a form of the word *burni*, 'burnished, darkly lustrous'; *cf.* Godefroy, 1, 707a, *bourné*
boutés: see *boucter*, above
bran (d'un poulet) 19: brawn, muscle, dark meat (of chicken); T-L, 1, col. 1126, *braon*
brasmes 29: ichth., a fish of the family *Sparidæ*, sea bream
Brehee, la 55: a variety of sauce (of fried onions, for salt meats); origin and meaning of the word unclear
broche 10, 43, brochette 43, broque 59: spit
brouet 1, 3, 20, 21, 22, 23, 24, 25, 27, 54, brouuet 66: broth; **Brouet d'allemaigne de char 21, Un ~ de**

III. Ingredients and Glossary — 99

canelle 20, ∼ de hongherie 54, ∼ rousset sur tel grain que vouldrez 21, ∼ de vergus 24, ∼ vergay 25, **Un soultil ∼ d'engleterre 23**

broye 8, broyez 12, 14, 56, bruyerés 61, broyé 19, 23, broyez 38, broyeez 20, 55: to grind, crush, pound

brun 4 (pain), 61 (pain), 64 (cuquere): brown, reddish brown, dark

bruyerés: see *broye*, above

buef: see *beuf*, above

bure 1, 3, 7, 8, 15, 17, 27, 30, 60, 63 burre 65: butter

cabillaut 61: ichth., *Gadus morhua*, cod

cambrelencq 16: chamberlain; **Une souppe de cambrelencq 16**

cameline 6, 15, 36 *subst.*, camelins 33, 37 *adj.*: cameline; **Une saulse cameline 6, Saulce non boullie ditte ∼ 36, Aux camelins 37**

canelle 2, 4, 6, 7, 8, 13, 16, 17, 20, 21, 22, 23, 29, 36, 43, 44, 52, 54, 55, 66: bot., *Cinnamomum verum*, cinnamon; **Un brouet de canelle 20**

cappon: see *chapon*, below

carpres 14, 27, 29: ichth., *Cyprinus carpio*, carp; **Un civet de carpres 27**

cecille 51: Sicily; **Vermiseaux de cecille 51**

chapon 50, cappon 62, chapons 56: capon; **Ung bouruet sur ung cappon rosti et ... becquet 62, Ung pignagoscé sur chapons 56**

char 4, 5, 9, 10, 11, 22, 60, 66, chars 9: flesh, meat; **Char de mouton 10, ∼ de porc fresche 9, ∼ de venoison 11**

charbon 16: coal, (hot) coals

chastaigne 23: chestnut

chaudel 3: caudle, a variety of prepared dish; **Un chaudel sur eulx pochiez 3**

chucquere 6, 7, 8, 12, 14, 16, 17, 19, 30, 49, 55, brun cuquere 64: sugar; Pegolotti describes six generally available sugars, of which the best is *zucchero caffettino*, which has *bruni bubgi di sopra*; chucqueré 50, chucquerez 53: sugared

chuyre 63: to cook (*cuire*)

civet 27: civet, on onion-based dish; **Un civet de carpres 27**

clou 6, 20, 21, 23, 29, 36, 39, 44, 52, 54, 56, 57, cloux 30, claux de ginofle 66: bot., *Eugenia caryophyllus*, cloves

cochon 54, 57: swine, pig, pork

commin 18, 48: bot., *Cuminum cyminum*, cumin

comminee 18: cumin dish, cuminade; **Une comminee de poisson 18**

connir 22: rabbit

confir 16: to steep, macerate (a foodstuff in a sweet substance)

contrefait 49: counterfeit, mock; contrefaictez 49: to counterfeit

coulez 29, 30: to strain, filter; Latham, fasc. 2c, 376c, *colare*, 'to filter, strain'; *REW*, §2035, *couler* < *colare*, 'filtrer'; *cf. coulich*, below

couleur 2, 5, 14, 27, 30, 54, coulleur 58: colour; couleurs 15: treatment, appearance, style

coulich 19: cullis, a variety of prepared meat broth, of subtle, homogenous texture, normally for the sick; **Un coulich de malades 19**; Gamillscheg, p. 263b, 'durchgeseihte Kraftbrühe': substantified adjective from *couler* + *aticius*; *cf. coulez*, above

craisse 58, crasse 64, gresse 43, 50: grease, fat; cras 26, gras 27, 28, 49, 50, 51, 53, crase 64, crasse 58, grasse 5: greasy, fatty

cresme 7, 8, 17: cream

cresson 28: bot., *Barbarea vulgaris* or *Nasturtium officinalis*, garden cress or watercress

cretonnee 46, 47: a variety of dish; **Cretonnee de fevez 47, ~ de pois nouveaux 46**

crevesches 42: freshwater crustacean of the genus *Cambarus*, crayfish

crottee 26: a variety of sops, 'lumpy'; **Une soupe crottee 26**

desmeller 65, desmellé 61, desmellez 45: to thin, make more liquid, by mixing into a liquid; Godefroy, 'disperser'

destempré 4, 23, 39, destemprés 58, destemprez 14, 38, destempreez 20: to infuse, macerate (so that an undesirable temperament is corrected); see *estrampés*, below

devers: par devers 31, 34: toward; T-L, 2, col. 1865, *par devers*: 'in der Richtung von, in der Richtung nach, gegen ... hin'

dilligamment 5, 7, 30, 46, 49, 53: attentively, assiduously

diner 64: to dine

dore 58, dorez 8, doreez 29: to gild

douch: see *sain*, below

dragié 16 (feminine): a spiced candy

duc 8: a variety of powdered spice mixture; see *poudre*, below

eaue: see *esve*, below

effueillié (persin) 21, 35, 42, 56: (of parsley, using) its leaves alone

egalment (sel) 5, 17, 30, 42: reasonably, judiciously, evenhandedly, (salt) to taste; (faictez feu) egalment 15: evenly

elle 58: wing (*aile*)

enfariner: see *farine*, below

engleterre 23: England; **Un soultil brouet d'engleterre 23**

ensaffrenné: see *saffren*, below

entremés 15, 29: a prepared dish, functioning as an interlude

esbrocher 43: to mount on a spit

escaille 8: shell (of egg)

eschauder 32, eschaudez 35: to pass through scalding water

escliffins 61: ichth., *Melanogrammus aeglefinus*, haddock

eslire 51, eslit 50: to clean of dirt

espic 23, 29, espicq 29: bot., *Lavandula spica*, aspic, lavender; perhaps spikenard

espices 1, 5, 5, 29, 39, 55, 66, 66, espices (communes) 27, espicez 24, 44, especes 66, espesses 64: spices

espressée: see *orenge*, below

essuer 50, 51, 57: to dry

estamine 2, 4, 6, 18, 19, 21, 23, 27, 30, 39, 40, 41, 44, 46, 54, 56, 57, 61, 62, 65, 66: a filter (usually of woollen cloth)

estamper (garlic) 61, (amande) 65, estampés (ozelle, amandes) 61: to pound, crush

estoupes 60: tow (tufts of wool, flax or hemp fibres); T-L, 3, col. 1409

estrampés 61: to infuse, macerate (to give a desirable temperament to); see *destempré*, above

esturgon 35: ichth., *Acipenser sturio*, sturgeon

❖ III. Ingredients and Glossary ❖

estuver 5: to stew
esve 1, 2, 3, 5, 9, 10, 11, 15, 17, 20, 23, 24, 25, 26, 27, 29, 30, 35, 42, 44, 52, eaue 58, 58, yauwe 61, 64, 66, yawe 62, yauw 66: water; esve rose 52: rosewater, a distillate of an infusion of rose petals
esventrés 14: to gut, eviscerate (a fish)
eulx: see *oef*
farine 49: flour; enfariner 32, enfarinez 8: to flour
farse 8, 12: stuffing, filling, composition, mixture; farsir 8: to stuff; **Pour farsir oes 8**
fevez 47: bot., beans
flans 12, 14: flans, low custard pies; **Flans de quaresme 12**
fleur (d'amidun) 12, 30, (de blé) 58: fine flour
foellez (petittez foellez de laurier) 29: (small laurel) leaves
fondant (fromage) 7, 8: very soft
forche 66: strength (of vinegar)
forque 64 *prep.*: except for, but only
fourboulir 66, fourboulés 64: to parboil; Godefroy, 4, 114a; *cf. ibid.*, 4, 64c
fourment 30: wheat
fourmentee 30, formentee 30: made of wheat (*fourment*), a variety of frumenty, a wheaten porridge or gruel; **Une grenee fourmentee 30**
foye 23, 33, 62, foyez 56: liver
frisiez 15, frissiés 63, fris 27, frit 15, frite 60, fritte 31, 32: to fry; see also *refrisent, suffrire*, below
fromage 7, 8, 25, 26, 49, 51, 53, fromaiges 51: cheese
froyé (pain) 5: to grind, crush; see also *gratuisié*
fumee (du brulé) 66: (burnt) odour

galles, en galles 49: in jest, as a joke; Godefroy, 4, 207b, 'réjouissance, plaisir, amusement; *par galle*: par plaisanterie'; **Rys en galles c'on dit "contrefait" 49**; T-L, 4, col. 64, 'Lustbarkeit, Vernügen'
garentine 44: galentine; **Lamproye a la garentine 44**
garingal 23, 29, 30: bot., *Cyperus longus*, galingale, galangal
gaune 61: yellow; gaunist 61: to make yellow
gellee 29: jelly, a jelled dish; **Gellee de poisson 29**
gernons 30, 46: treads (of an egg)
gingembre 2, 4, 6, 12, 13, 16, 18, 20, 21, 22, 23, 24, 25, 29, 30, 36, 39, 41, 43, 44, 46, 52, 54, 55, 56, 57, gengembre 61, 62, 65, 66: bot., *Zingiber officinale*, ginger
ginofle: see *clou*, above
glaires 62: egg whites; see also *blans*; *cf. moyeulx*, below
grain 20, 20, 21, 21, 22, 24, 24, 25, 25, 29, 46, 54, 54, 55, 56, 57, 57: meat, as the principal foodstuff of a prepared dish
graine 2, 4, 6, 12, 20, 21, 22, 23, 24, 29, 36, 39, 43, 44, 52, 54, 56, 57, grains [sic] de paradis 29: bot., *Amomum melegueta*, grains of paradise
gras: see *craisse*, above
graté (fromage) 53, gratté (fromage) 7, 49, 51: grated; see also *gratuisié*
gratuisié (pain) 53: grated; see also *graté* and *froyé*
greil 6: grill
grenné 53: a variety of prepared dish; **Une grenee fourmentee 30, Potage grenné 53**

gresse: see *craisse*, above
guelle 15, guele 43: mouth, maw
hanap 48, hanaps 58: stemmed goblet; a measure of volume
haricocq 45: a variety of mutton dish; **Un haricocq de mouton 45**
harlé 6, 21, 27, 36, 39, 43, 56: toasted
hechiet 62: chopped; elsewhere *hachié, hachiez*
herbes 9, 10: herbs
hongherie 54: Hungary; **Brouet de hongherie 54**
huille 13, 15, 32, oille 60: (olive) oil

incontinent 66: immediately

jansce 41: a variety of ginger sauce, jance; **Jansce de lait de vache 41**
jaunet 39: yellowish, a qualification of a dishname

keuwe 15: tail

lait (d'amandes) 12, 14, 18, 22, 28, 50, lait (de vache) 30, 41, 46: milk; **Poree en lait d'amandes 28, Jansce de ~ de vache 41**
lamproye 43, 44: ichth., *Lampetra fluviatilis* or *Petromyzon marinus*, river or sea lamprey; **Lamproye 43, ~ a la garentine 44**
lard 21, 24, 25, 45, 46, 55, 56, lart 65, 66: fat meat of a pig, bacon; lardé 10, lardés 64, 66: barded or interlarded with pieces of fat pork; see also *sain*, below
laurier 29: bot., *Laurus nobilis*, laurel, bay laurel
lesches 16, lesques 61: slices (of bread)
liant 54: bound, thick (of liquid preparation)

lievre 64, 66: hare; **Potage de lievre 64 & 66**
linge 15: linen cloth
lombarde 7: Lombard; see *votte*, below
louce 30: large spoon, ladle; louchiés 66 *fem. subst.*: spoonsful, ladlesful
loie, 59, loye 59: to bind, tie (*lier*)
luchs 13: ichth., *Esox lucius*, pike; see also *becquet*, above
lyemesolles 57: snails (mod. *limaçons*); **Lyemesolles sur tout bon grain 57, a garnish**

macis 6, 29, 30, 54: bot., *Myristica fragrans*, ground from the lacy aril between the outer husk and inner shell of the nutmeg seed, mace; *cf. mughettes*, below
meismes 42 *adv.*: self
menut 62: small
menuyse 13: small fry, the young of fish
mirés, oes mirés 63: fried or poached eggs; **Oes mirés a le sause 63**
mistion 58, mistions 59: mixture; T-L, 6, col. 99
moillon 15, 30: middle, centre
mort: cuire (ble) a mort 30: to cook (wheat) until disintegrating; *cf.* cuire (anguillez) a mort 12, with a literal sense; see also *pouris*, below
mostarde 11, moustarde 1, 10: mustard
mouton 10, 45: sheep; **Un haricocq de mouton 45**
moyeulx 5, 17, 23, 24, 25, 30, 46, moyelx 57, moyeux 53, moioeufs 58, mioefz 8, 41: egg yolks; *cf. glaires, blans*, above
mughettes 43, mughettez 44, muscades 22, 29, 30: bot., *Myristica fragrans*, nutmeg; *cf. macis*, above

❖ III. Ingredients and Glossary ❖

noyrois 13: Norse; **Pastez noyrois 13**: Norse Pasties, a prepared dish

oef 49, 62, 63, oes 3, 5, 7, 8, 23, 24, 25, 30, 41, 46, 53, 57, 63, oeufs 58, oels 17, oex 65, eulx 3: egg; see also *glaires* and *moyeulx*, above; **Oes mirés a le sause 63**

ognons 21, 22, 27, 45, 55, 63, oygnons 63: onions

oille: see *huille*, above

oisiel 58, oysiaulz 59, oysiaux (de riviere) 66: bird, (water) fowl

oison 54, oyson 59: gosling; see also *auwe*, above

onde (bouillir une onde) 1, 18, 20, 28, 43, 46, 52, 53: to bring to a boil, boil briefly

ordonnance (in the *Incipit*): ordering, directions

orenge 15: orange; *orenge espressee*, orange juice

otant 66 *pron.*: as much (mod. *autant*)

ozelle 61: sorrel, macerated, as a source of a green colorant

paiele (saininoire) 58: (dripping) pan; payelle 26, 62, 66: (frying) pan; in 66, made of either iron or earthenware

pain 2, 4–6, 9, 14, 16, 18, 21, 24–27, 36–41, 43, 44, 46, 53, 54, 56, 57, 61, 63, 64, 66: bread

pains 58: to paint

paradis: see *graine*, above

parcuire 2: to finish cooking, cook completely

passer 63, 66, passés (imperative) 64, passé 5, 9, 24, 25, 36, 43, 66, passeez 20: to strain, filter; explicitly, with *parmy l'estamine*: passer 62, 65,

passez (imper.) 18, 39, passés (imper.) 61, 66, passé 2, 4, 6, 19, 21, 23, 27, 30, 40, 41, 44, 46, 54, 56, 57

pasté 5, 14: a thick mixture (such as would serve as a pie filling), a dish of meat-paste; pasté 65, 66, pastés 65, 66, pastez 13, 14, patez 13: pasty, pie; **Un pasté en pot 5, Pastez noyrois 13, ~ de pouchins 65**; pasté 51: pastry, pastry dough

pau 64, pauch 59: little; see also *poy*, below; (mod. *peu*: see *peu* in 62, 65, 66)

persin 3, 8, 9, 10, 21, 25, 35, 42, 45, 56, 62: bot., *Petroselinum crispum* or *hortense*, parsley

picquant (verius) 62: sharp, pungent, tart; *cf. poingnant*, below

Pignagoscé sur chapons, ung 56: a variety of rich, hot sauce for capons

pinte 66: (roughly) pint

plais 33, 34, plays 31, 32: ichth., *Pleuronectes platessa*, plaice

poingnant 37: penetrating, dominating (said of a flavour); *cf. picquant*, above

pois 29, 46, 48, 55, poix 48: bot., peas (pureed); **Cretonnee de pois nouveaux 46**

poisson 13, 14, 15, 18, 29, 44, 60, 61, poissons 61: fish; **Pour cuire un poisson en trois manieres 15 & 60, Une comminee de ~ 18, Gellee de ~ 29, Blanque sause non boulie ... a ~ 61**

poivre 30: bot., pepper; poivre long 6, 23, 24, 39, 44, 54, 57: *Piper longus*, long pepper; poivre noir 40, 55: *Piper nigrum*, black pepper; poivre chault 11: a sort of pepper sauce;

Poivre chault noir 40, Un ~ jaunet 39
poix: see *pois*, above
polioel 10, 45: bot., *Mentha pulegium*, pennyroyal; T-L, 7, col. 138, 'Flöhkraut'
pommes 17: apples
porc 9, 23, 55, porcq 65: pig, swine; see also *pourchellet*, below
poreaulx 55: bot., *Allium porrum*, leeks
poree 28: stewed herbs, vegetable greens; **Poree en lait d'amandes 28**
potage 31, 53, 64, 66: pottage, a dish prepared by stewing in a pot; **Potage grenné 53, ~ de lievre 64 & 66**
potee 52: a variety of prepared dish (see comment to Recipe 52); **Potee de poullaille 52**
pouchins 65, 65: chicks; **Pastés de pouchins 65**
poudre 61, 62, pouldre 58, poure 48, 61, 65: powder (of a particular spice); poure, fine poure 61: powder (of an unidentified spice or spice mixture); pourldre de duc 8: a particular mixture of ground spices; pouldrez (imperative) 53, 55, pouldré 10: to grind, reduce to powder
poulet 1, 19, 58, poullet 58, 59, poulez 46: chicken; **A faire .i. poullet aler rosti sur le table 58, A faire chanter ledit ~ mort 59**; see also *pouchins, poullaille*
poullaille 22, 52: poultry
pourbouliez 28, pourboulir 2: to parboil
pourchellet 59: piglet
pouris (de cuire) 55: disintegrating (said of onions, from being boiled); see also *mort*, above

poy 1, 5, 6, 12, 14, 19, 25, 43: little; see also *pau*, above
premiés 63 *adv.*: first, in the first place; *cf. premiers* 1
puree 29, 48, 55: puree (of peas); purer 46: to puree (peas)
purer 42, 63, purez 17: to drain

quaresme 12, 48, 50: Lent; **Flans de quaresme 12, Soupe de ~ 48**
quarte 48: quart; quartron 30: the fourth part of a hundred, *i.e.*, twenty-five; Godefroy, Cotgrave

raye 33, rayes 33: ichth., of the family *Rajidæ*, ray or skate
refrisent 13: to fry (furthermore); refrit (persin) 3: fried (parsley), fried by itself; perhaps sauteed, 'parfried'
ris 12, rys 49, 50, 51: rice; **Rys en galles 49, ~ en gresse 50**
riviere (oysiaux de) 66: river, aquatic (birds)
Robert, une barbe Robert 1: a variety of sauce
rocques 61: ichth., *Rutilus rutilus*, roach (a carp-like fresh-water fish)
rose: see *esve*, above
rost (noun) 59: roast meat; mettre en rost 64: to roast
rostir 10, 16, 18, 43, 66, rostissant 10, 15, rostez (imperative) 1, rostissiés (imperative) 66, rosti 4, 15, 58, 59, 61, 62, 63, rosty 15, rostie 32, 58, 60: to roast (meat, fish, bread); see also *tostees*
rouge: see *vin*, below
roux 21, 54: dark (reddish) brown; rousset 21, 27, 61: russet (coloured); **Brouet rousset sur tel grain que vouldrez 21**

❖ III. Ingredients and Glossary ❖

rouget 31: ichth., *Mullus surmuletus*, red mullet

rys: see *ris*, above

sablon 29: (a bed of) sand

sachiés 66: to withdraw, pull out

saffren 1, 2, 4, 5, 6, 9, 12, 14, 17, 18, 22, 23, 25, 27, 29, 30, 39, 46, 48, 57, 58, saffran 61: saffron; ensaffrenné 51, 53, ensafrenee 61: coloured with saffron

saille, sailles: see *sauge*, below

sain 20, 66: fat, grease; sain de lard, lart 21, 24, 45, 46, 55, 56, 66: pork fat, grease; sain d'auwe douch 66: rendered goose grease

saininoire: paiele saininoire 58: dripping pan (beneath a roast)

salures 55: salted meats

sang 43, 44, 54: blood; (couleur) sanguine 54: blood-red

sauge 10, 25, saille 10, sailles 9: bot., *Salvia officinalis*, sage; T-L, 9, col. 62, *saille*, 'ein Küchengewächs, Salbei'

se 7, 29, 61, 62, 65, 66 conj.: if (mod. *si*)

silion 30: bot., *Anthriscus cerefolium*, chervil

solles 32: ichth., *Solea solea*, sole

soultil 23: subtle, consisting of fine particles; **Un soultil brouet d'engleterre 23**

soupe 26, 48, soupes 3, souppe 16, souppes 48, 62: sops; **Une souppe de cambrelenque 16, ~ crottee 26, ~ de quaresme 48**

sourmetaine 30: bot., *Laserpithium siler* or *Siler montanum*, laserwort, hartwort; Godefroy, 7, 394a; Cotgrave,

'*sermontain*, Siler Mountaine, bastard Loveage'; Huguet, 7, 142a, *surmontain*, 'sorte de plante'; T-L, 9, col. 532, with ref. to the *Grant herbier*, Rosskümmel

suffrire 45, suffrisiez 8, 17, 20, 21, 52, suffrit 22, 24, 25, 46, 54, suffris 46, 55, 56: to fry lightly or partially, brown, sear, sautee (likely derived from *soubs+frire*)

telle 27, 44: baking dish, a relatively deep vessel likely of earthenware and perhaps resembling a rounded roofing tile; *REW*, 8614, *tegela; Godefroy, 7, 662c, 'sorte de vase très évasé'; T-L, 10, col. 150, 'Tiegel, irdenes Gefäss'; cf. *Menagier*, ed. Pichon, p. 276, *boulés en pot ou en telle*, glossed by the editor as 'teille, vase de terre'

temprer 6, 9, 16, 61, 63, 66, tempret 61, tempré 2, 4, 18, 24, 27, 41, 43, 46, 56, 57, 64: to temper, modify the temperament of a foodstuff or mixture

tenche 14, tenches 29: ichth., *Tinca tinca*, tench

tostees 62: slices, pieces of toast; see also *rostir*

touppie 58: to turn about, rotate; Godefroy, 7, 746c, *topier*: 'tourner, tournoyer'

tuille 15: (roofing) tile

turbot 29, 34: ichth., *Scophthalmus maximus* or *Rhombus maximus*, turbot

vache (lait de) 30, 41, 46: cow

venoison 4, 11: venison, game meat

verd: see *vert*, below

Glossary

vergay 25: 'cheery green,' bright green, yellowish green; **Brouet vergay 25**

vergus 1, 2, 3, 9, 10, 20, 21, 24, 25, 36, 38, 41, 42, 45, 48, 52, 54, 56, 57, 64, verius 61, 62, 63, 65, 66, vertius 61, vierius 66: verjuice; vergus renouvellé 10: a sort of sauce; **Brouet de vergus 24**

vermeille: see *vin vermeille*, below

vermiseaux 51: vermicelli, very fine spaghetti; **Vermiseaux de cecille 51**

vert 10, 32, 34, 61, verd 15, vers 51, verde 61, 65: green; see also *vergay*, above

viande 58, 65, viandes *Incipit*: meat, food

vin 1, 4, 5, 7, 11, 16, 19, 20, 21, 24, 25, 26, 27, 29, 31, 35, 36, 39, 42, 43, 44, 45, 48, 52, 54, 57, 66: wine; vin rouge 6, 56, vin vermeille 66: red wine

vin aigre 2, 4, 6, 10, 13, 35, 40, 42, 44, 54, 56, 57, 64, 66, vinaigre 36, 37, 39, 61, 63, 66, vin esgre 66: vinegar

Votte lombarde, une 7: a prepared dish, a sort of custard; Godefroy, 8, 299c, *volte*: 'omelette, crêpe'

yauwe: see *esve*, above

ysope 10, 45: bot., *Hyssopus officinalis*, hyssop

❖

IV. Appendices

A. Table of the Recipes in the *Vivendier* and Concordances in the *Enseignements* and *Viandier*

New f°	Orig. f°	Rec. #	Recipe name	Concordances
154r	cxl	1.	Une barbe Robert	[*Viandier* 163]
		2.	Assisse d'anguillez	
		3.	Un chaudel sur eulx pochiez	
154v		4.	Assisse de venoison	
		5.	Un pasté en pot	
		6.	Une saulse cameline	
155r	cxli	7.	Une votte lombarde	
		8.	Pour farsir oes	
		9.	Char de porc fresche.	
155v		10.	Char de mouton	*Ens.* 4; *Viandier* 3
		11.	Char de venoison	*Ens.* 15; *Viandier* 7
		12.	Flans de quaresme	*Enseignements* 55
		13.	Pastez noyrois	*Enseignements* 55
156r	cxlii	14.	Aultre maniere de pasté et de flans	*Enseignements* 55
		15.	Pour cuire un poisson en trois manieres	
156v		16.	Une souppe de cambrelencq	
		17.	Un amplummus	
		18.	Une comminee de poisson	*Ens.* 33; *Viandier* 75
		19.	Un coulich de malades	*Viandier* 90
157r	cxliii	20.	Un brouet de canelle	*Viandier* 14
		21.	Brouet rousset sur tel grain que vouldrez	*Viandier* 16
		22.	Brouet d'allemaigne de char ...	*Viandier* 22
157v		23.	Un soultil brouet d'engleterre	*Viandier* 24
		24.	Brouet de vergus	*Viandier* 25
		25.	Brouet vergay	*Viandier* 26
158r	cxliiii	26.	Une soupe crottee	
		27.	Un civet de carpres	
		28.	Poree en lait d'amandes	[*Viandier* 153]
158v		29.	Gellee de poisson	*Ens.* 26; *Viandier* 68
159r	cxlv	30.	Une grenee fourmentee	*Viandier* 63
159v			**Chapittre de poissons**	
		31.	Plays	*Viandier* 133

		32. Solles	*Viandier* 135
		33. Rayes	*Viandier* 136
		34. Turbot	*Viandier* 137
		35. Esturgon	*Viandier* 146
160r	cxlvi	**Chapittre de saulces**	
		36. **Saulce non boullie** ditte cameline	*Viandier* 155
		37. Aux camelins	*Viandier* 156
		38. Aux blans	*Viandier* 157
		39. **Saulces boulliez** — d'un poivre jaunet	*Viandier* 164
		40. Poivre chault noir	*Viandier* 165
		41. Jansce de lait de vache	*Viandier* 166
		42. Crevesches	*Viandier* 151
160v		43. Lamproye	*Viandier* 69
		44. Lamproye a la garentine	*Ens.* 25; *Viandier* 70
161r	cxlvii	45. Un haricocq de mouton	*Viandier* 4
		46. Cretonnee de pois nouveaux	*Viandier* 11
		47. Cretonnee de fevez	*Viandier* 11a
		48. Soupe de quaresme	
161v		49. Rys en galles c'on dit "contrefait"	
		50. Rys en gresse	*Viandier* 71
		51. Vermiseaux de cecille	
		52. Potee de poullaille	
162r	cxlviii	53. Potage grenné	
		54. Brouet de hongherie	
		55. La brehee	
162v		56. Ung pignagoscé sur chapons	
		57. Lyemesolles sur tout bon grain ...	

	58.	A faire .i. poullet aler rosti sur le table
163r cxlix	59.	A faire chanter ledit poullet mort ...
	60.	Un poisson ou une piechs de char ... que une partie soit rostie, ... [*incomplete*]
163v	61.	Blanque sause non boulie ... a poissons Item ... gaune; Item ... verde; ... Faire les dites sause sentir les aux
	62.	Ung bouruet sur ung cappon rosti Et pareillement sur becquet ...
	63.	Oes mirés a le sause
164r cl	64.	Potage de lievre
	65.	Pastés de pouchins
164v	66.	Potage de lievre

B. Juxtaposition of the *Vivendier,* the *Viandier* and the *Enseignements*

This second Appendix presents a juxtaposition of recipes in the *Vivendier* and the *Viandier*[1] where there is some apparent correspondence between the texts. In most cases the *Viandier* is represented by the reading found in the manuscript copy in the Bibliothèque Mazarine, Paris (MAZ): while the copy in the Archives Cantonales du Valais, Sion (VAL) represents the oldest known version — a sort of proto-*Viandier* — and that of the Biblioteca Vaticana, Rome (VAT) the largest (and most recent) manuscript compilation of the *Viandier*, MAZ seems generally to dispose of relatively old texts in the traditional canon though at a relatively late date. In this the *Vivendier* resembles MAZ even if clearly without the desire of the latter's compiler to reproduce the whole of that canon.

Wherever, for purposes of comparison, a variant reading is inserted below, the manuscript source of that variant is also indicated.

Additionally, certain of the recipes in the *Enseignements*[2] bear sufficient similarity with those of the *Vivendier* to be reproduced here as well.

Vivendier text	*Viandier* texts

Chy commenche un vivendier et ordonnance pour apparillier pluiseurs manierez de viandes. | *BN Cy comence le Viandier Taillevent maistre queux du Roy nostre sire, pour ordenner les viandes qui cy aprés s'ensuivent.*

Enseignements. Vezci les enseingnemenz qui enseingnent a apareillier toutes manieres de viandes.

[1.] **Et premiers, pour faire une barbe Robert: prenez un poy de belle esve, et le mettez boullir avoec du bure; et puis ...** | 163. [a boiled sauce] *VAT La barbe Robert, autrement appelee la Taillemaslee.*

---

[1] The edition used for this comparison is *The Viandier of Taillevent. An Edition of all Extant Manuscripts*, ed. Terence Scully, Ottawa (University of Ottawa Press), 1988. The manuscript *sigla*, VAL, MAZ, BN and VAT, are those employed in that edition.

[2] The edition used for the texts of the *Enseignements* is that of Carole Lambert, edited as part of her Ph.D. Thesis for the Université de Montréal, currently in press; the recipe number is according to that edition. Also indicated, in parentheses, are the line numbers of the recipe in the edition of Grégoire Lozinski in *La Bataille de Caresme et de Charnage*, Paris (Champion), 1933; Appendice I, pp. 181–187.

[10.] Char de mouton soit mis rafreschir pareillement pour estre la char plus blanche, puis mis rostir en la broche, et lardé de persin et de sauge quant elle sera my cuitte, et arossee de vin aigre ou de vergus en rostissant; ou soit mis boullir en esve avoec persin, ysope, saille, polioel et autrez bonnes herbes; et mengié a la sauce vert ou au vergus renouvellé. Le pouldré a la moustarde.

3. MAZ Boulitures de grosses chairs comme beuf, porc, mouton. Cuysiez en aigue et sel et maingier aux hauls blans ou a verjus reverdi, et y mecter a cuyre pierressy, saulge, ysouppe; et la salee maingier a la moustard.

> *Enseignements*, 12 (ll. 39–41). Por char de mouton. Char de mouton fresche, en yver e en esté, doit estre cuite o sauge e o ysope e o parressil, e mengié a la sause verte; la salee a la mostarde. E qui en veut de rosti des costez, il la puet mengier a la devandite savour.

[11.] Char de venoison soit cuitte en vin et en esve, et mengié au poivre chault; le salé a la mostarde.

7. VAT Venoison de sanglier frez. Cuit en vin et en eaue; a la cameline et au poivre aigret; le salé, a la moustarde.

> *Enseignements*, 22–25 (ll. 89–92). Touz conins e touz lievres sont bons en pasté. Connins en rost, au poivre chaut ou aigre, rostiz o tout les piez. Nul lievre n'en est bon en rost, fors en esté. E si est bon en pasté, menuement lardé. Veneison fresche, au poivre chaut; la salee a la mostarde.

[12.] Pour faire flans de quaresme : cuissez anguillez a mort, puis hostés les arrestez et tout le noir, puis le broyez en un mortier; gingembre, graine et saffren, deffait de lait d'agmandes ou poy de fleur d'amidun ou de ris, et de ce faictez vostre farse; et au dreschier, chucquere largement.

152. BN Viande de Quaresme. Pour faire flaons et tartes en quaresme. ... Item, en autre maniere: prengnés anguilles et en ostés les testes les getés et les queuez ossi, et broiés bien le remanant avec saffren deffait d'un pou de vin blanc; puis emplés vos flans et sucrés du sucre quand ils seront cuis.

> *Enseignements*, 55 (ll. 166–169). Se vos volez fere flaons en caresme, prenez anguilles, si en ostez les arestes quant il seront cuites; puis si les breez bien en un mortier, e i metez un poi de gingembre e un poi de safren e de vin. E de ce poez fere flaons ou tartes ou ...

❖ IV. Appendices ❖

[13.] Pour faire pastez noyrois : prenez menuyse de luchs u d'aultre bon poisson, cuit, taillié par lopins, canelle et gingembre deffait de vin aigre ; et faictez petis patez ; aucun les refrisent en huille.

Enseignements, 55 (ll. 170–173). Por fere pastez norreis, prenez menuise de luiz ou d'autre pesson e ce boulliez; puis tailliez par morseaus comme dez, e i metez gingembre e canele, e destrempez d'un poi de vin; puis en fetes vos pastez. E les fetes petiz e frisiez en uile.

[14.] Pour faire aultre maniere de pastez et de flans : prenez tenche, carpres et d'aultre bon poisson, l'esventrés, sy le broyez tresbien en un mortier avoec mie de pain et un poy de saffren pour donner couleur ; destemprez tout de lait d'amandes ; chucquere largement et au dreschier.

Enseignements, 55 (ll. 174–178). Se vos volez fere pastez qui aient savor de formage, ou flaons en caresme, prenez les leitenches de carpes ou de luiz e pain; puis breez tout ensemble e destrempez de let d'alemandes. E se vos voiez qu'il est trop blanc, si i metez un poi de safren. E de ce povez fere vos pastez e flaons en Caresme, si avront savor de formage.

[18.] Pour faire une comminee de poisson : prenez du lait d'amandes et du pain blancq tempré dedens sans rostir, commin, gingembre et saffren ; passez tout parmy l'estamine, faictez boullir une onde ; qui ne soit trop cler ne trop espés ; et jettez par dessus vostre poisson, quel qu'il soit.

75. [a thick, meatless pottage] *VAL Conminee de poisson. Cuit en yaue ou fruit [frit] en huile; affinez amandez deffetes du boullon ou de puree ou d'eaue boullie, et en faitez lait; fetez boullir; affinez gingembre, commin, deffait de vin et de verjus, metez boullir avec vostre lait; pour maladez, y fault du succre; dreciez sur vostre grain d'anguille.*

Enseignements, 48 (ll. 129–130). Se vos volez fere comminee de pesson, prenez commin e alemandes, si les breez, e destrempez d'eve clere e colez, e metez dedenz le pesson.

[19.] Pour faire un coulich de malades : prenez le bran d'un poulet bien cuit, bien broyé et passé parmy l'estamine, deffait du boullon ; faictez boullir ; vin un poy, sel et chucquere.

90. [a sickdish] *MAZ Colis d'ung poulet. Cuisiez le poulet tresfort en aigue, puis le broyer tout et les os aussi, puis deffaicte de vostre boillon et couler; et y mecter du sucre; et ne soit pas tropt lyant.*

[20.] Pour faire un brouet de canelle : cuisiez tel grain que vouldrez en vin et en esve, et despechiez par lopins et suffrisiez en beau sain ; puis prenez amandes bien laveez sans peller, broyeez et passeez, destempreez de bon boullon, gingembre, clou et graine, deffait de vergus ; faictez tout boullir ensamble, et votre grain avoecquez, une onde seulement.

[21.] Pour faire brouet rousset sur tel grain que vouldrez : prenez ognons tailliez par roelles et persin effueillié — sy le suffrisiez en beau sain de lard ; prenez pain harlé deffait de bon boullon et passé parmy l'estamine, gingembre, canelle, clou, graine, vin et vergus ; faictez boullir tout ensamble, et vostre grain comme dessus ; et soit bien brouet roux.

[22.] Pour faire brouet d'allemaigne de char de connir, de poullaille ou autre : soit despechié par pieches et suffrit avoec ognons menu hachiez ; prenez lait d'amandes grant foison, gingembre, canelle, nois muscades, graine et saffren et faictez tout boullir ensamble avoeques bon boullon, et jettez par dessus vostre grain.

[23.] Pour faire un soultil brouet d'engleterre : prenez grosses chastaigne cuittez, bien pelleez, moyeulx d'oes crus, foye de porc, broyé tout ensamble, destempré de boullon ou d'esve tieve, passé parmy l'estamine ;

14. [a thick pottage] MAZ Brouet de cannelle. Cuisiez vostre poulaille en aigue et en vin, puis despeciez par quartiers et frissez en sain de lart; et prener amandres seches sans pillez et de la cannelle grant foison, broyez, couler et deffaicte de vostre boillon et faicte boulir avec vostre grain, et du verjus, avec gigimbre, giroffle, grainne de paradis; et soit tresbien lyant.

16. [a thick pottage] MAZ Brouet rousset. Prener tel grain conme vous voudrois et oignons par rouelles et parsin effuellé, frisiez en sain de lart; puis deffaictes foyes [VAT pain et foyes] de boillon de beuf et mecter boulir avec vostre grain; puis affiner gigimbre, cannelle, giroffle, graine, fleur de cannelle, deffaicte de verjus; et qu'il soit bien roux.

22. [a thick pottage] MAZ Brouet d'Alemaigne. Prener chart de connins ou de poulaille et les despeciez per morceaulx et des oignons menuz menusiez, et frissiez en sain; puis affinez amendres grant foison, deffaicte de boillon de beuf et de vin et faicte boulir avec vostre grain; puis affiner gigimbre, cannelle, giroffle, graine de paradis, noix minguetes, et ung pol de saffrain qu'il soit sur jane coulour et lyant, deffaicte de verjus.

24. MAZ Soubtifz brouet d'Angleterre. Prener chastaignes cuites et pilez, et moyeuf d'euf cuis en ung pol de foye de port [VAL cuis et ung pou de foie de porc; VAT cuis en vin, un pou de faye de porc]; broyer tout ensamble, destramper d'ung pol d'aigue tiede et coulez;

❖ IV. Appendices ❖

prenez gingembre, canelle, clou, graine, espic, poivre long, garingal et saffren, et faictez tout boullir ensamble.

puis affinez gigimbre, cannelle, graine, garingal, poivre long, espit et saffrain pour donner couleur, et faicte boulir tout ensamble.

[24.] Pour faire brouet de vergus : cuisiez tel grain que vouldrez en esve, vin et vergus le plus ; et pain passé, tempré en vergus, et moyeulx d'oes, espicez — gingembre, graine et poivre long ; faictes boullir tout ensemble, bien assavouré de sel, et qu'il passe le vergus ; jettez par dessus vostre grain bien suffrit en beau sain de lard.

25. VAT Brouet de verjus de poullaille ou de tel grain comme vous vouldrez. Cuisiez en vin, en eaue et en verjuz tellement que le goust du verjus passe tout l'autre; puis broyez gingenbre et des moyeulx d'oeufz tous cruz grant foison et passez tout parmy l'estamine ensemble et mettez boullir, puis gectez sur vostre grain quant il sera friolé —et mettez du lart au cuire pour luy donner goust.

[25.] Pour faire brouet vergay : cuisiez tel grain que vouldrez en vin et en esve ou bon boullon de beuf, et du lard pour donner goust ; prenez pain passé deffait dudit boullon, persin, sauge et moyeulx d'oes, fin fromage qui voelt, et vergus, gingembre et saffren un poy pour faire vergay ; faictez tout boullir ensemble ; et jettez par dessus vostre grain — mais qu'il soit bien suffrit.

26. VAT Brouet vertgay. Cuisiez tel grain comme vous vouldrez en vin et en eaue et en boullon de beuf, et de lart pour luy donner goust, puis convient bien frioler vostre grain; puis affinez gingenbre, saffren, persil, ung pou de sauge qui veult, et des moyeulx d'oeufz tous cruz, et du pain, tout passé parmy l'estamine, deffait de vostre boullon, et i fault ung pou de verjuz; et de bon froumage qui veult.

[28.] Pour faire poree en lait d'amandes : prenez anguille pourbouliez, et poree de bettez et de cresson, puis tirez vos anguilles et poree dehors ; ayez lait d'amandes et du plus gras de vostre boullon, faictes boullir en un pot, assavouré qu'il soit de bon sel ; mettez vostre poree dedens et anguilles boullir une onde, puis si les drechiez chaudement.

153 VAT Poree de cresson [unnamed in MAZ]. Prenez vostre cresson et le faictes boullir et une pongnee [MAZ une poingnis] de bettes et mettés avec, puis la miciez et friolés en huille et puis la mettez boullir en lait [MAZ en lait d'amandres] si vous la voulez telle [MAZ ; et saler appoint]; ou en charnage, en l'eaue de la chair ou au frommage, ou toute crue sans riens y mettre, se vous la voulez ainsi. Et est bonne contre la gravelle.

[29.] Gellee de poisson — carpres, tenches, brasmes, turbot et aultre bon poisson : soit bien affaittié et cuit en vin et en esve, puis le tirez hors du boullon sur une belle nape pour esgoutier quant il sera bien cuit ; prenez espices — gingembre, canelle, clou, graine, saffren, espicq, garingal, deffaict de puree de pois ; mettez tout boullir ensamble ; et se vous veez qu'il soit trop espés, sy le coulez devant le feu ; puis dreschiez vostre grain em plas bien clers et luisans, et jettez par dessus chaudement ; puis assez vos plas en lieu froit sur le bel sablon ; aucun y mettent des amandes pelleez et des petittez foellez de laurier doreez et argenteez, et en servent comme d'un entremés.

Pour faire .lx. escuelles de gellee y fault :
.x. onches de grains de paradis ;
item, .vi. onches de macis ;
item, .iii. onches de nois muscades ;
item, .iiii. onches de gingembre ;
item, une onche de clou ;
item, .vi. onches de canelle ;
item d'espic et garingal, .ii. onches de chascun.

68. [an *entremets*] VAT Gelee de poisson a lymon et de chair. Mettez le cuire en vin et en verjus et en vinaigre, et aucuns y mettent de l'eaue ung pou ; puis prenez gingenbre, canelle, girofle, grainne de paradiz, poivre long, et deffaictes de vostre boullon et passez parmy l'estamine, puis mettez boullir avec vostre grain ; puis prenez feulles de lorier, espic, garingal et maciz et les liez en vostre estamine sans la laver, sur le marc des autres espices, et mettez boullir avec vostre grain, et le couvrez tant comme il sera sur le feu, et quant il sera jus du feu si l'escumez jusqu'a tant qu'il sera drecié ; et puis quant il sera cuit, si purez vostre boullon en ung net vaissel de boys tant qu'il soit rassiz ; et mettez vostre grain sur une nappe blanche, et se c'est poisson si le pelez et nettoiez et gectez voz pelleures en vostre boullon jusqu'a tant qu'il soit coullé la derniere foiz, et gardez que vostre boullon soit cler et net ; et puis dreciez vostre grain par escuelles ; et aprés remetez vostre boullon sur le feu en ung vaissel cler et net et faictes boullir, et en boullant gectez sur vostre grain et pouldrez, sur vos platz ou escuelles ou vous avez mis vostre grain et vostre boullon, de la fleur de canelle et du macis ; et mettez voz plas en lieu froit pour prendre. ...

Enseignements, 53 (ll. 154–160). Se volez fere gelee de pesson, esquerdez le pesson e depechiez par pieches, c'est assavoir carpes e tenches, bresnes e tourboz ; e metez cuire en vin pur e fort ; puis prenez canele, gingembre, poivre lonc, garingal, espic e un poi de safren, puis breez e metez tout ensemble ; e quant vous l'osterez du feu, si en traez le pesson par escueles e verseiz sus ; e se vos veez qu'il soiet trop espés, si le colez ; e lessiez refredier jusques au matin, e lors si le prenez autressi comme gelee.

❖ IV. Appendices ❖ 115

[30.] Pour faire une grenee fourmentee : mettez du ble cuire a mort, puis coulez l'esve hors nettement et laissiez reffroidier ; puis ayez lait de vache nouvellement trait et le mettez boullir en un noef pot ; et quant il est sur le point de fremir, jettez vostre fourment dedans petit a petis en remuant dilligamment ; et quant tout est ens, tirez le pot arriere du feu ; puis ayez moyeulx d'oes bien batus, et les gernons nettement hostez, saffren et fleur d'amidun, et tout ce passé parmy l'estamine ; faictez boullir tout ensamble tant qu'il soit si espés que le louce se puist tenir droite ou moillon ; puis le tirez arriere du feu et jettez dedens bure et sel egalment ; et qu'il soit de belle couleur.

Pour faire .xx. escuelle de grenee formentee, fault un quartron d'oes ;
item, de garingal, de macis, de cloux, de gingembre, de saffren, de nois muscades, de silion, de poivre, et sourmetaine — de chascune une once ;
item, une livre de chucquere, une livre d'amigdum, et demie livre de bure.

63. [an *entremets*] MAZ *Fromentee. Prener froument, espailliez et lavez tresbien, puis le mecter cuire et le purer; puis bouler lait de vaiche une onde et mecter vostre froument dedans et mecter boulir et remuer souvent; puis quant ilz sera bien reffroidiez, fillez dedans moyeuf d'euf bien batus et ung poul de saffrain et succre assés par dessus le pout; et aulcuns y mectent espices; et doit estre bien janet et lyant.*

[31.] Plays doivent estre aparilliés par devers le dos au dessoubz de l'oreille, et bien laveez ; cuitte comme un rouget ; a sausse de vin et de sel ; ou, qui en voet en potage, soit fritte.

133. [a flat sea-fish] VAT *Pleys. Affaictiez par devers le doz dessoubz [BN au dessoz de] l'oreille, bien lavee, cuitte come ung rouget, a saulse de vin et de sel; et qui veult en potaige, soit cuite [BN frite] sans farine.*

[32.] Solles doient estre apparilliez et cuitte comme plays, et mengié a la saulce vert; et, qui voelt, soit rostie sans eschauder, ou fritte en huille sans enfariner.

135. MAZ Soit eschaulder et apparoilliez conme plays, et maingier a la saulce verde, au chaudumé; et la rotiez sur le gril et au verjus d'usille.

VAT Solles. On les doit eschauder et puis cuire et affiner come la pleiz en eaue, et mengier a la saulce vert; et en rost, qui veult, sans eschauder, au verjus; et escorchent aucuns le dos; et la fricte, [BN sans ferine et] sans eschauder, en huille.

[33.] Rayes soient apparilliez par le nombril, et gardez bien le foye; sy despechiez la raye par pieches et cuisiez comme la plais, puis la pellez; et mengiez aux aux camelins.

136. VAT Roye. Appareilliee par endroit le nombril et gardez le foye, et la despeciez par pieces et la cuissiez come une pleiz, et puis la pelez; et la mengiez tyede aux aulx camelins. Et du foye aucuns font des tostees et mettent du frommage de gain bien tenve pardessus; et est bonne viande et bien friande.

[34.] Le turbot soit cuit et apparillié comme une plais, et puis pellez par devers le dos; a la sauce vert.

137. VAT Turbot. Appareillié et cuit come une pleiz et puis pelé par devers le doz; et doit estre par pieces; et mengié a la saulce vert ou en souz.

[35.] Esturgon: eschaudez, et fendez par le ventre et le teste fendez et copez en deux et tous les aultres tronchons que se puellent fendre fendus, et cuis en vin et en esve — que le vin passe; quant il est cuit, mettez reffroidir; et soit mengié au persin effueillié et au vin aigre par dessus.

146. [a sea-fish] VAT Esturjon. Eschaudez le et le fendez par le ventre, et la teste couppee et fendue en deulx et tous les autres tronçons fendus qui se pourront fendre [MAZ qu'il se peuvent fendre fender], et soit cuit en vin et en eaue, et que le vin passe, et puis le traiez et laissiez reffroidir; et aprés le mettez en vinaigre et en persil.

[36.] Saulce non boullie dicte cameline: canelle, gingembre, clou et graine et pain passé harlé bien noir, deffait de vergus, vin et vinaigre.

155. [an unboiled sauce] MAZ2 Saulse cameline. Broyés gigimbre et cannelle grant foison, giroffle, graine de paradis, mastic, poivre long qui·l veult; et puis coulez pain halés, tramper en vin aigre, et atramper tout apoint et salez.

❖ IV. Appendices ❖

[37.] Aux camelins se font pareillement, mais il y fault dex aux poingnant le vinaigre.

156. [an unboiled sauce] MAZ2 Haulx camelins. Broyer cannelle, haulx et pain; deffait de vin aigre.

[38.] Aux Blans: bien broyez, et mie de pain blancq, destemprez de vergus.

157. [an unboiled sauce] VAT Aulx blans. Broyez aulx et pain et deffaittes de verjus.

[39.] Saulces boulliez — d'un poivre jaunet: prenez pain harlé destempré de vinaigre et de vin, et le passez parmy l'estamine; espices — saffren, clou, poivre long, gingembre et graine; faictez boullir tout ensamble.

164. [a boiled sauce] MAZ2 Broyer poivre, gigimbre, saffrain, pain alez, deffaicte de vin aigre et la mecter boulir; et ung pol de giroffle et du verjus.

[40.] Poivre chault noir: pain brullé noir deffait de vin aigre et passé parmy l'estamine; faictes boullir avoec poivre noir.

165. [a boiled sauce] MAZ2 Poivre noir. Broyer gigimbre, poivre ront, pain bruler, deffaicte de vin aigre [VAL, MAZ, BN et de verjus] et faicte boulir.

[41.] Jansce de lait de vache: pain blanc tempré en lait, et mioefz d'oes passé parmy l'estamine, et gingembre blancq deffait de vergus; faictez tout boullir ensamble.

166. [a boiled sauce] BN Jance au lait de vache. Broiés gingembre, moieux d'oeufs, deffaites de lait de vache, et faites boullir.

[42.] Crevesches: on les doit bien laver et cuire en un pot bien couvert sans esve, avoec du vin — ou du vin aigre et de l'esve ou du vergus — et du sel egalment; et laissiez bien boullir si qu'il se puist escumer de lui meismes, puis les purer et tenir que bien couvertes chauldement; puis mengier au sel et au vin aigre ou persin effueillié par dessus.

151. [a sea-fish] VAT Escrevices de mer. Cuites en vin et en eaue, ou mises ou four; et mengiez en vinaigre.

117. [a fresh-water fish] VAT Escrevisses. Cuites en eaue et en vin [BN en eaue et en vin aigre]; [BN mengiez] au vinaigre.

[43.] Lamproye: on la doit faire saignier par la guele, et hoster la langhe; et y convient boucter une brochette de bois dedens pour mieulx saignier — et gardez bien le sang car c'est sa gresse — puis le faitte esbrocher comme une anguille, et rostir en une broche bien delié; puis prenez gingembre, canelle, graine, mughettes et un poy de pain harlé, tempré en vin et passé, et faictez boullir ensamble une heure ou tant; mettez vostre lamproye boullir avoecquez toute entiere une onde seulement; et ne soit pas trop noire vostre saulce.

69. [an *entremets*] VAT Lamproye fresche a la saulce chaude. Soit seignee par la gueulle et luy ostez la langue, et convient boutter une broche pour mieulx seigner, et gardez bien le sang car c'est la gresse, puis la convient eschauder comme une anguille et rostir en une broche bien deliee, et doibt estre mise et percee travers en guise de une ou de deux; puis affinez gingenbre, canelle, girofle, grainne de paradiz, noix muguetes et ung peu de pain brulé trempé ou sang et en vinaigre et, qui veult, ung pou de vin, et en deffaites tout ensemble et faictes boullir une onde, et puis mettez vostre lamproye avec toute entiere; et ne soit mie la saulce trop noire. . . .

[44.] Lamproye a la garentine: faictez sangnier vostre poisson comme dessus, et gardez le sang; puis le cuisiez en esve, vin et vin aigre, et, quant elle sera cuite, tirez le ariere du feu et laissiez reffroidir; puis le mettez sur une belle nappe; prenez pain brullé deffait de vostre boullon, passé parmy l'estamine, et du sang de vostre lamproye; faictez boulir tout ensamble et gardez bien qu'il n'arge; puis le versez en une telle, et le mouvez tant qu'il soit refroidié; prenez espicez — gingembre, clou, graine, canelle, mughettez, poivre long — desmellez ensamble, et mettez vostre poisson dedens.

70. [an *entremets*] VAT Lamproye en galantine. Seignez la comme devant, gardez le sang, puis la mettez cuire en vinaigre et en vin et en ung pou d'eaue; et quant elle sera cuite si [MAZ l'ostés hors du feu] la mettez refroidier sur une nape; puis prenez pain brulé et le deffaictes de vostre boullon parmy une estamine, et puis mettez boullir le sang avec, et mouvez bien qu'il ne arde; et quant il sera bien boullu, si versez en ung mortier ou en une jatte nette et mouvez tousjours jusquez ad ce qu'il sera refroidié; puis affinez gingenbre, fleur de canelle, giroffle, grainne de paradis, noys muguettes, poivre long et deffaictes de vostre boullon et mettez dedans; et puis vostre poisson avec, dedans une jatte comme devant, et la mettez en vaissel de fust ou d'estain: si avez bonne galentine.

Enseignements, 25 (ll. 144–153). Se vos volez fere galentine a la lampree, prenez pain levei e breez e le metez cuire ovec le sanc de la lampree e bon vin blanc, e soient enleuvés [encuvés?] en cel vin meismes, e i metez grant foison de poivre e de sel assez soffisnment; puis prenez les lamproiez e metez sus une nape pour refredier, e puis prenez du pain, si le breez e destrempez de vin aigre. E quant vos avrez ce fet, si le colez parmi un saaz, e puis ce metez en une paele clere e fetes boullir, e mouvez tousjors que il n'aurse; puis le metez refredier e le movez bien; e puis prenez vos poudres de gingembre, de canele e de girofle fetes, si metez par avenant sus vos lamprees, e cuillés, e metez [en] vos bariz.

[45.] Pour faire un haricocq de mouton : mettez le par lopins tout cru suffrire en beau sain de lard avoec ognons hachiez menu, vin et vergus et bon boullon, persin, polioel, ysope ; faictez tout bien boulir ensamble.

.4. VAT *Hericoc de mouton. Prenez vostre mouton et le mettez tout cru soubzfrire en sain de lart, et soit despecié par menuez pieces, des ongnons menuz meiciez avec; et deffaictes de boullon de beuf, et y mettez du vin et du verjus, et macis, ysope et sauge; et faictes bien boullir emsemble.*

[46.] Cretonnee de pois nouveaux : soient cuis jusques au purer, puis suffris en beau sain de lard ; prenez lait de vache et le boulez une onde en un noef pot ; ayez pain blancq tempré oudit lait, gingembre et saffren, tout passé parmy l'estamine ; puis ayez moyeulx d'oes bien batus et les gernons hostez, jettez dedens sur le point de fremir et vos pois dedens en remuant dilligamment ; puis ayez vostre grain — poulez par pieches — suffrit en sain de lard, et boullis une onde avoecques ; puis dreschiez chaudement.

11. [a thick pottage] VAT *Cretonnee de poys nouveaulx. Cuissiez les jusques au purer et puis les purez, et les frisiez en sain de lart; puis prenez lait de vache et le boulliez une onde, et mettés tremper vostre pain dedans le lait; et faictes gingenbre et saffran brayer et le deffaictes de vostre lait, et faictes boullir; et puis prenez poulles cuites et eaue et les despeciez par quartiers et les frisiez, puis mettez boullir avecques; puis traiez arriere du feu et y fillez grant foison de moyeulx d'oeufz.*

[47.] Cretonnee de fevez se fait pareillement.

11A. VAT *Cretonnee de feves nouvelles. Ainsi comme celles de poys cy devant.*

[50.] Rys en gresse : soit bien eslit et lavé, puis mis essuer devant le feu ; et quant il est bien secq, mettez le cuire en bon boullon gras de chapon ou aultre, et en quaresme en lait d'amandes ; bien chucqueré au dreschier.

71. VAL *Ris. Cuire en gresse, a jour de char. Eslisiez, lavez en yaue chaude, metez essuier contre le feu, metez cuire en lait de vache fremiant; broiez saffren pour rougir, deffait de vostre lait de vache; metez dedans du gras et du boillon.*

❖

C. *Contre pestilence* ...

Following the last recipe of the *Vivendier*, which ends at the foot of f° 164v — this being the last folio of the gathering containing the culinary collection — the subsequent gathering opens (at f° 165r; old foliation, *cli*) with a set of instructions on ways to counteract the plague. This regimen is declared to have been been composed by Master Jacques Despars, the same physician whom we saw contribute a filler, at the foot of f° 153v and just before the text of the *Vivendier*, on how to settle an upset stomach. Because the four pages of advice in the regimen incorporate many details of contemporary doctrine touching upon foods and foodstuffs, and consequently bear to some extent upon the culinary practice that is illustrated in the *Vivendier*'s recipes, we provide a transcription and translation of the doctor's counsel here.[3]

[f° 165r] Pour se garder contre pestilence: du conseil maistre Jaque des Pars.

[1.] Pour se preserver de pestilence on se doit garder de toutes choses qui eschaufent le sanc, comme font sel, salures fortes, espices, fortes saulses, aux, ognons, poriaus, moustarde, fors vins, claré, ypocras, estuves, bains, tout traveil de corps, et courous.

[2.] *Item*, on se doit garder de fruis crus nouviaux et de tous laitages et d'oeus et de poissons qui ne sont point bien frecs.

[3.] *Item*, on se doit garder de converser avec malades, et de repairier en lieu ou il a eu des infecs, et de recevoir en son hostel leur lis, vestures ou couvretures.

[4.] *Item*, on se doibt garder de touttes viandes estouppans, comme de pain sans levain, de feves, de coles, de chars de porc, de buef, de cherf, de tripes, de saulsices, d'andouilles, de poissons de limon, de moust, et de buvrages tourbles.

[f° 165v][4] [5.] *Item* on doit user de nettes et legieres viandes comme de pain de sain fourment, d'yaue de poulaille au vertjus, avoecq ung peu de saffran, ou d'yaue de viau ou de puree de pois ou de blans mengiers d'amandes et de porees de bettes et de bouraces.

[6.] *Item*, de chars de pouchins ou de glines [*sic*] ou de capons ou de perdris ou de faisans ou de widecos ou de plouviers ou d'aloettes ou

---

[3] For other plague tractates, see A. C. Klebs and E. Droz, *Remèdes contre la peste*, Paris (Droz), 1925; A. Coville, "Ecrits contemporains sur la peste de 1348 à 1350," *Histoire littéraire de la France*, Vol. 37, Paris, 1937, pp. 325–90; and R. Simonini, *Maino de Maineri ed il suo Libellus de preservatione ab epydimia*, Modena (Orlandini), 1923.

[4] Centred at the top of the page and separated from the text, as if a rubric, are the words *Pour soy user etc.*

de cabri ou de connins ou de mouton ou de viau de d'oeus mols nouviaus ou de soles ou de rougés ou de becqués ou de perques ou de vendoises ou d'escrevices et de roisins de quaresme.

[7.] *Item*, on doit mengier tant sa char comme son poisson au vertjus de grain vieil avec .i. pou de vin aigre et en mettre cuire avec sa char et son poisson le tierc d'un gobelet.

[8.] *Item*, on doibt boire petit vin franchois blanc ou claret fort tempré d'yaue boullie.

[f° 166r][5] [9.] Tant que est au fait de medecine, est bon de prendre une fois ou .ij. la sepmainne .vi. ou .vij. pilulles communes au vespres a l'aler couchier, de .vij. en le dragme.

[10.] *Item*, est bon de[6] laver sa bouche, ses mains et ses narines tous les matins de bon vin aigre avoec le double d'yaue rose ou de fontaine.

[11.] *Item*, est bon de prendre une fois le sepmainne vers minuit ou au matin bien matin le gros d'une feve de fin triacle avec .iij. louchiés d'yaue d'escavieuse.

[12.] *Item*, les jours ensieuvans est bon de prendre tous les matins une louchié de la poudre qui s'ensieut sus une tostee de pain mouillie en vin blanc ou claret comme on prent poudre de duc: ...

[13.] *Item*, est bon se saignier de .ij. mois en .ij. mois en quantité de .ij. petites palettes de la vaine du ceur ou dou foye, puis en .i.[7] brach puis en l'autre, et prennez du dextre.

[14.] [f° 166v] Le regime dessusdit est bon contre pestilence pour toutes personne excepté qu'on ne doit point sangnier femmes grosses ne enfans de soubs .xiiij. ans ne donner pillulles communes, etc.

Per balneo ou pour laver ses ghanbes ou bras quant on se grate, et pour les purifier, etc.: ...

Pour purifiier le gros sancq qui est cause au corps de creature de plusieurs apostume, claux ou escaumpine: ...

[f° 167r][8] Poudre laxative a boire au matin: ...

Pour aller a cambre: ...

[f° 167v] *Item*, pour homme ou pour femme garir de dur ventre ou[9] enflet: ...

Item, pour mal de fourchielle: ...

Item, pour playe trop toés close: ...

Item, pour vraye medechine contre arsure ou escaudure: prenés oefs durs quits en chendre, puis s'en ostés le blanc — se ne prenés que le

---

[5] Centred at the top of the page is the old foliation: *Clij*.
[6] The word *de* is inserted above the line by means of a caret.
[7] The numeral is inserted above the line.
[8] Centred at the top of the page is the old foliation: *Cliij*.
[9] *ou*: ms., *en*.

myoefs[10] — se le mettés en une paiielle sur feu, se le mouvés d'une louchette, s'en iscera de l'ole; cheste olle mettés en ung voire, et est le plus vraye medechine c'on puet trouver. Aprouvés est.

[f° 168r][11] *Item*, encontre mal de fourchielle ou contre flumes: ...

Item, pour le dos enflees: ...

Item, contre mal de fourchielle: ...

Item, encontre mal de costet: ...

Item, pour cheuls que ne peuent user leur viande: ...

Item, pour cheuls qui ne peuent mengier par desgoustemens: ...

[f° 168v] *Item*, pour bras ou gambes endormy: ...

Item, pour garir festure: ...

Item, contre flumes: ...

Item, pour main ou bras endormis: ...

[f° 169r][12] *Item*, pour mal des rains: ...

Item, remede contre une apostume dedens le corps et par impedimye, et qu'on ne scet plus que faire: ...

Item, tresbon ongement pour saner vielles[13] plaies et maladies en gambes: ...

[f° 169v] *Item*, chy parolle de goute qui tient et vient es hancques de caude cause: ...

[f° 170r][14] *Item*, pour mal de fourchielle: ...

Item, pour mal des oreilles[15]: ...

Item, pour piere qui est en le vessie brisier: ...

Item, pour garir gravielle: ...

Item, pour gambes enflees: ...

Item, pour gambes enflees: ...

Item, pour mal de dens: ...

[f° 170v] *Item*, pour mal de gambes enflees ou crapeuses: ...

Item, pour mal de gambes: ...

Item, pour purgier l'estomacq: ...

[f° 171r][16] *Item*, pour le mal du chief: ...

Item, contre fievre: ...

Item, pour medechine de fluemes: ...

---

[10] ms.: *lemye oefs*.

[11] Centred at the top of the page is the old foliation: *Cliiij*.

[12] Centred at the top of the page is the old foliation: *Clv*.

[13] ms.: *viesses*.

[14] Centred at the top of the page is the old foliation: *Clvj*.

[15] Before *des oreilles*, the words *de costes* were written then crossed out.

[16] Centred at the top of the page is the old foliation: *Clvij*.

❖ IV. Appendices ❖

To protect oneself against the plague, as counselled by Master Jacques des Pars.

[1.] *To protect oneself from the plague, one should avoid all things that warm the blood, as do salt, heavily salted meats, strong spices, sauces with onions, leeks, mustard, strong wines, claré, hipocras, hot baths, baths, any physical work, and anger.*

[2.] Likewise, *one should avoid raw fresh fruit and any dairy product and eggs and fish which are not very fresh.*

[3.] Likewise, *one should avoid talking with sick people, and entering anywhere there has been infection, and receiving in one's dwelling their beds, clothing or bedding.*

[4.] Likewise, *one should avoid any constipating foods, such as unleavened bread, beans, cabbages, pork, beef, stagmeat, tripe, sausages, chitterlings, fish, limon, must and opaque beverages.*

[5.] Likewise, *one should eat clean, light foods such as good wheaten breat, chicken broth with verjuice, with a little saffron, or veal broth or pea puree or almond White Dish and purees of beet greens and borage.*

[6.] Likewise, *chicken and hen, or capon, partridge, pheasant, woodcock, plover, lark, kid, rabbit, mutton, veal, fresh, uncooked eggs, sole, red mullet, pike, perch, dace, crayfish and currants.*

[7.] Likewise, *one should eat both meat and fish with a mash of old verjuice grapes and a little vinegar, and cook these in a third of a goblet of the same.*

[8.] Likewise, *one should drink little French white or claret wine, much diluted with boiled water.*

[9.] *On the topic of medicine, it is good once or twice a week to take six or seven common pills, [of the size of] seven to the dram, in the evening going to bed.*

[10.] Likewise, *it is good to wash one's mouth, hands and nostrils every morning with good vinegar mixed with twice as much rosewater or fountain water.*

[11.] Likewise, *it is good once a week around midnight or very early in the morning to take a bean's amount of treacle with three spoonfuls of water from a dug well.*[17]

[12.] Likewise, *on the following days it is good every morning to take a spoonful of the following powder on a slice of toast moistened in white or claret wine as Duke's Powder*[18] *is taken:* [A medical recipe in Latin follows.]

---

[17] The word *escavieux* is unattested in any Old French dictionary, but Godefroy shows a verb *escaver*, "extraire en creusant" ["to dig out"].

[18] For this *poudre de duc* see the comment to Recipe 8 in the recipe collection, above.

[13.] *Likewise, it is good to be bled every other month to the amount of two small porringers from the heart or liver vein, then from one arm then the other, [beginning with (?)] the right.*

[14.] *The above regimen is good against the plague for anyone, except that pregnant women and children under fourteen years should not be bled, nor receive common pills, and so forth.*[19]

Likewise, *to bathe or to wash one's legs or arms when they are scratched and to cleanse them, and so forth:* ...

To purify coarse blood which brings about various abscesses, carbuncles or running sores[20] *in the body:* ...

A powder for a laxative to be drunk in the morning: ...

To help going to the toilet: ...

Likewise, *to cure a man or woman of a hard or swollen belly:* ...

Likewise, *for stomach ache:* ...

Likewise, *for a wound that has healed dirty*[21]*:* ...

Likewise, *for effective medicine against burns and scalds: get eggs hard cooked in the coals, remove the white and take only the yolks, putting them in a pan on the fire and stirring them with a small spoon, and oil will come out of them; put this oil in a glass: it is the most effective medicine that can be had. It is proven.*

Likewise, *against stomach ache or against phlegm:* ...

Likewise, *for a swollen back:* ...

Likewise, *against stomach ache:* ...

Likewise, *against a stitch in the side:* ...

Likewise, *for those who cannot digest their food:* ...

Likewise, *for those who are off their food:* ...

Likewise, *for pins and needles in the arms or legs:* ...

Likewise, *to cure a fistula:* ...

Likewise, *against phlegm:* ...

Likewise, *for pins and needles in the hand or arm:* ...

Likewise, *for back pain:* ...

---

[19] A break in the text occurs here. Clearly this paragraph closes the section entitled *Pour se garder contre pestilence*. Although no rubric follows here, the nature of the material changes.

[20] A nasal is written for the middle of this word, even though Godefroy (3, 358a) shows only the word *escaupine*, "démangeaison, nom d'une maladie, p.-ê. la gale."

[21] The word in the manuscript, *toes*, is likely either a form of the verb *tooillier* (Godefroy, 7, 745a, "salir, souiller") or perhaps a poorly written version of *trop tost esclose*.

♦ IV. Appendices ♦

Likewise, *a treatment against an abscess within the body and from the plague, and when nothing else works:* ...
Likewise, *a very good ointment to treat old wounds and leg ailments:* ...
Likewise, *here, gout in the hip of a warm origin:* ...
Likewise, *for stomach ache:* ...
Likewise, *for earache:* ...
Likewise, *to break bladder stone:* ...
Likewise, *to cure kidney stone:* ...
Likewise, *for swollen legs:* ...
Likewise, *for swollen legs:* ...
Likewise, *for toothache:* ...
Likewise, *for a disease of swollen or scabby[22] legs:* ...
Likewise, *for sore legs:* ...
Likewise, *to purge the stomach:* ...
Likewise, *for headache:* ...
Likewise, *against fever:* ...
Likewise, *medicine for phlegm:* ...

The contents of the Kassel manuscript copied immediately after the collection of culinary recipes continues to direct the reader on the use of foodstuffs — meats, fish, fowl, condiments (herbs and spices), liquids — but for more specifically medical purposes. In the half-dozen folios after f° 164v there are two sorts of counsel: a plague tractate, and a series of directions on how to treat particular, rather common ailments.

The first medical "recipe", of a rather universal nature, is by no means unique to our collection. As a *genre*, the advice on "How to Protect Oneself from the Plague" can be found in a multiplicity of variants across Europe from the middle of the fourteenth century onwards. Especially following the great plague of 1347–48 physicians were called upon desperately to advise any effective means by which one might avoid this mortal infection. Serious recurrences of the infection struck Paris in 1418–19 and Flanders and Artois (the home of Jacques Despars and probable origin of our manuscript) in 1435–38. Learned physicians responded to persistent pleas for help by formulating such monitory catechisms as that of Jacques Despars which our compiler has copied here.

Because much of such counsel touched upon the food that could or should be consumed in times of plague, it is not at all surprising to find Dr. Despars's

---

[22] The term *crapeux* is defined by Godefroy (2, 357a) as "atteint de la *crape*," which in turn is defined as a "sorte de maladie". Tobler-Lommatsch (2, col. 1014), however, defines *crape* as "Mauke an der Fessel der Pferde".

small tractate, *Pour se garder contre pestilence*, copied alongside the *Vivendier*. His famous masterwork, the commentary on Avicenna's *Canon*, shows a remarkably pervasive and highly instructive interest in foods, their nature and effects. Here in this present tractate, many of the paragraphs offer advice on food that is similar to that which, in the form of standard sickdish recipes, is frequently incorporated as a matter of course into ordinary culinary recipe collections. In the *Vivendier* itself only three recipes, Recipes 17, 18 and 19, can be seen as fulfilling this function. The manuscript's compiler may well have intended Dr. Despar's tractate as a reasonable complement to the preceding recipe collection.

Interestingly, the *Du fait de cuisine*, whose text dates from a generation before the *Vivendier* and which already contains an extensive section of sickdish recipes, also saw a three-stanza ballade entitled *Contre l'ympydimie* appended to it on a blank folio by some prudent individual — whether cook, physician or owner/compiler of the manuscript.[23]

Contemporary medical analysis of the late-medieval plague determined that in its essence it was a product of excessively warm and moist humours: when affected by the pestilence one had a fever and one sweated. Therefore, clearly and logically, it was dangerous to consume any foodstuff, or to participate in any activity, that was perceived as being particularly warm or humid; and most especially one ought to eschew any foodstuff or activity that was marked by a temperament that combined the two of these qualities together.

The first paragraph of Dr. Despars's "recipe" lists those things that could instil warmth to a dangerous degree: salt and heavily salted meats, spices and heavily spicy mixtures (to which are later added spiced wines), and garlic, onions and leeks.

The second paragraph likewise cautions against consuming those things that were looked upon as being excessively moist in nature: fruits, dairy products and fish that might be "corrupting". Fish in themselves normally partook of the nature of their environment, but the tendency, the less fresh a fish is, for it to yield more and more fully to its moist nature was readily apparent.

The third paragraph reveals a suspicion that proximity to an infected person or to his intimate property could be dangerous.

The fourth paragraph warns against foods that, as a contemporary physician would categorize them, are oppilative. While variously warm, cool, dry and moist, even to only moderate degrees, these foodstuffs carried the threat of constricting the bowels of the individual at any time, but dangerously so in time of plague. Manifestly the digestive track had to remain fully open in order to flush and expel

---

[23] See *Chiquart's "On Cookery". A Fifteenth-Century Savoyard Culinary Treatise*, ed. Terence Scully, New York, Berne & Frankfurt (Peter Lang), 1986, pp. 120–122.

those ill humours from the body. We have already seen an inexplicit reference to *limon* in Recipe 29, above: this substance, found on the skins of certain fish and known empirically to be effective in making a jelly, clearly possessed the potential of causing a similar congealing and consequent obstruction within the bowels.

In the fifth and sixth paragraphs the doctor returns at length to the question of foodstuffs, here those that are most beneficial in time of plague. The guiding principle in this prescription is that the foods be as close in temperament to the human complexion as possible: slightly warm and slightly moist. The meats, fowl and fish, almonds, greens and egg yolks constitute a list of what were held to be the most desirable foodstuffs in the late Middle Ages. In particular fowl, participating in the warm, moist nature of air itself, were good foods, and of these, because of their very habitat in the wild — wild creatures being in general warmer than their domestic equivalents — certain game birds were preferred.

The seventh paragraph amounts to a general safety clause: being cool and dry, verjuice and vinegar could exert a corrective influence upon any meat, fowl or fish that might be *unhealthily* warm or moist.

Paragraph ten incorporates advice that was most commonly given by physicians during a plague: vinegar, of a cool and dry temperament, was ubiquitously recommended as a means to check the warm and moist contagion. Handkerchiefs soaked in vinegar were regularly held over the nose by anyone who had to venture beyond the safety of his own house.

The series of paragraphs that follows Dr. Despars's plague tractate, on the treatment of specific ailments, frequently as well involve the use of what we would look upon as foodstuffs. Such medical recipes being beyond the scope of this edition, we have offered a number of rubrics from this section merely for interest. The curious reader will note the frequency with which contemporary patients seem to have complained of digestive problems; the advice attributed to Dr. Despars on settling an upset stomach, copied immediately ahead of the *Vivendier*, is in very good company in our manuscript.

D. Summary Bibliography

This Bibliography is minimal, listing only the most important primary sources for late-medieval culinary recipes in the French language. For critical studies of these recipe collections, and of the field of medieval French and European food and cookery in general, the reader can usefully consult the comprehensive Bibliography in Bruno Laurioux, *Le règne de Taillevent*, Paris (Publications de la Sorbonne), 1997, pp. 383–411.

Enseignements: Paris, Bibliothèque nationale, ms. lat. 7131, ff° 99va–100r; ed. Carole Lambert, *Trois réceptaires culinaires médiévaux: Les Enseingnemenz, les Doctrine et le Modus. Edition critique et glossaire détaillé*, Ph.D. Thesis, Université de Montréal, 1989 (in course of publication). Also ed. Grégoire Lozinski in *La Bataille de Caresme et de Charnage* (Bibliothèque de l'Ecole des Hautes Etudes), Paris (Champion), 1933; Appendix I, pp. 181–187.

Viandier: ed. Terence Scully, *The Viandier of Taillevent. An Edition of all Extant Manuscripts*, Ottawa (University of Ottawa Press), 1988. Also ed. Jérôme Pichon and Georges Vicaire, *Le Viandier de Guillaume Tirel, dit Taillevent. Nouvelle éditon augmentée et refondue par Sylvie Martinet*, Paris (H. Leclerc & P. Cormuau), 1892; repr. Geneva (Slatkine), 1967.

Menagier: Paris, Bibliothèque nationale, ms. fr. 12477; ed. Georgine E. Brereton and Janet M. Ferrier, *Le Menagier de Paris*, Oxford (Clarendon Press), 1981; the fifth Article of the second Distinction: "*Or convient maintenant monstrer des appareilz des viandes dessus nommees.*" Also Paris, Bibliothèque nationale, ms. n.a.fr. 6739; ed. Jérôme Pichon, *Le Ménagier de Paris, traité de morale et d'économie domestique composé vers 1393 par un bourgeois parisien*, 2 vols., Paris (Crapelet), 1846; repr. Geneva (Slatkine), 1970.

Chiquart: Maistre Chiquart Amiczo, *Du Fait de cuisine* (Savoie, 1420); Sion, Bibliothèque cantonale du Valais, Supersaxo MS S103; ed. Terence Scully, "Du fait de cuisine de Maistre Chiquart (1420)," *Vallesia*, 40 (Sion, Switzerland), 1985, pp. 101–231. Also translated by the editor as *Chiquart's "On Cookery". A Fifteenth-Century Savoyard Culinary Treatise*, New York, Berne & Frankfurt (Peter Lang), 1986.

Recueil de Riom: Paris, Bibliothèque Nationale, latin 6707, ff° 184v–188r; ed. Carole Lambert, *Le Recueil de Riom et la Manière de henter soutillement. Un livre de cuisine et un réceptaire sur les greffes du XVe siècle*, Montréal (CERES), [1988].

❖ IV. Appendices ❖   129

Vivendier: Kassel, Gesamthochschul-Bibliothek Kassel, 4° Ms. med. 1, ff° 154r–164v; this edition.

Anglo-Norman "A": *Coment l'en deit fere viande e claree*; British Library, MS Addl 32085, ff 117v–119v; ed. Constance B. Hieatt and Robin F. Jones, "Two Anglo-Norman Culinary Collections Edited from British Library Manuscripts Additional 32085 and Royal 12.C.xii," *Speculum*, 61 (1986), 859–882; Collection "A", pp. 862–866.

Anglo-Norman "B": [untitled]; British Library, MS Royal 12.C.xii, ff° 11r–13r; c. 1320–1340; ed. Constance B. Hieatt and Robin F. Jones, "Two Anglo-Norman Culinary Collections Edited from British Library Manuscripts Additional 32085 and Royal 12.C.xii," *Speculum*, 61 (1986), 859–882; Collection "B", pp. 866–868.

❖

❖